ABOVE US
ONLY SKY

ABOVE US ONLY SKY

Tales of the Kansas Homegrown

**Matt Farmer, Kent Farney, Bob Johnson
Jim Baker, Jim Captain**

Copyright © 2024 Matt Farmer

Cover photo by Ray Cottingham 1972.

DEDICATION

We dedicate this book to Herb Conley (1950-1972)

"Thank you, Herb. There would probably have never been a Kansas Homegrown without you."

ACKNOWLEDGMENTS

Our book could not have been written without the myriad contributions from fellow skydivers, friends and family. Special thanks to BA, Barb and Ron Luginbill, Mike Larson, Gregg Hackett and Skratch Garrison for improving the details, accuracy and dates obscured by the passage of time.

We appreciate the time, effort and suggestions offered during the book development, especially by Pam Bird, Cathy Shaw, Rick Shaw, Jackie Bird, Mike Holstein and Mike Larson.

Ray Cottingham graciously permitted his superb photographs from the era to accompany our text and thereby improve our book tremendously. Thank you, Ray.

So many unnamed photographers reflect the generous sharing between like spirits within the skydiving community, of their moments in space and time. Their photos enrich our book, and we thank them.

The unbelievable expertise, patience and countless hours expended by Richard Weaver, who formatted, edited and changed this dream into reality, cannot be overstated. Thank you is not enough.

TABLE OF CONTENTS

TALES OF THE
KANSAS HOMEGROWN

PREFACE

This is the story of a few young men who during the turbulent 1960's and '70's bonded into a small tribe of skydivers known as the "Kansas Homegrown," devoted to skydiving and the art of freefall relative work. It is, by the nature of its subject, at times a story of reckless, even irresponsible behavior. Skydiving was, arguably, the most extreme of what would later come to be called "extreme sports."

The development of skydiving coincided with a period in American history when social norms were relaxed enough that people felt they could "do their own thing." Jobs were plentiful; gas was cheap. It was a wonderful time to be young and lucky enough to catch the front edge of humans learning to use parachutes so they could freefall together.

Freefalling was a magical experience that created a fringe community of like-minded extremists who quickly expanded the frontiers of the new sport. The Kansas Homegrown were just such extremists.

As I say, this story is about a small band of dedicated freefall relative workers from Kansas. It is not a history or factual account of the development of skydiving or freefall relative work. Some of it, we're sure, did not happen in exactly the way remembered or depicted. Incredibly, however, much of it did.

PROLOGUE

Perspectives

In the early days, right after World War II, skydiving was called "sport parachuting." The activity was organized in clubs, mostly by some of the thousands of discharged WWII paratroopers the army had trained. The paratroopers' rule-bound focus was on jumping out of the plane and riding the parachute to the ground, not freefalling through the sky.

Skydiving

Something quite unexpected happened as the memory of the war years and the paratroopers faded into history. A distant echo of the pre-war barnstorming days of aviation appeared. In those days (1920's), parachutes had only just been developed. Barnstormers sometimes used parachutes as part of their shows.

At first, barnstormers just climbed out on the wing in flight, pulled the release mechanism on their parachutes and let the deploying chutes pull them off the wing and under the already open chutes.

It was during these barnstorming days, however, that a few barnstormers began jumping off the wing and falling earthward before finally deploying the parachute. Soon they were thrilling crowds by delaying longer and longer. What they learned to do by delaying the parachute opening was to "freefall." Freefall was thus born of daredevils and retains that reputation even though modern parachuting equipment and techniques have pretty much controlled the risks of learning.

That was not always the case. If you wanted to learn to freefall in the 1950's or 60's, you did it pretty much the same way the barnstormers had done it in the 1920s, by doing longer and longer freefall delays.

After a few short 5 and 10 second delays came the landmark fifteen second delay. It was on this jump the student first reached "terminal velocity" (the fastest speed an object will reach in freefall regardless of how long it falls). At terminal velocity, air resistance exactly matches the pull of gravity and speed becomes constant. It feels like riding on a soft supporting bubble of air. The first thing to learn to become a skydiver is how to relax and ride the bubble without spinning or washing around.

After a few fifteen second delays, the student was cleared to make longer freefalls. How long one could delay opening the parachute depended on the altitude one jumped from. Common jump altitudes were 7500 ft for a 30 second delay and 10,500 ft for a 50 second delay. Jumps from larger aircraft, especially for relative work, were from 12,500 ft for a full 60 seconds of freefall.

If you wanted to advance after finishing your 15 second delays, you asked more experienced jumpers to freefall with you and you kept your eyes open and your wits about you when they did. In this way, if you had the right stuff, you might eventually learn enough to be accepted as a skydiver. If not, you were welcome to hang around the drop zone and make an occasional parachute jump until you got bored or scared and quit. It was not egalitarian or inclusive, but it never (as it might have given that it was a male-dominated community) turned into something like *The Lord of the Flies*. Instead, skydiving became a brotherhood.

Pat and Jan Works, a literate California skydiving couple, did much to promote the idea of a skydiving brotherhood with their popular newsletter *RWUnderground*. Their later book, *United We Fall*, contains the most accurate and complete account of the development of skydiving and freefall relative work (RW).

Relative work itself is not hard to understand. In freefall, a person will not accelerate or decelerate relative to others freefalling at the same time unless the amount of drag imposed by the resistance of the air on the person is changed. It appears to one in freefall that others in freefall near them are simply floating in the sky. Freefalling skydivers on long delays found they could do "relative work" by controlling their body shape and position to speed up, slow down or move laterally relative to each other (hence, the name relative work).

Relative work gives one an unimaginable sense of flying. Flying in the way we dream of flying as children, not flying a machine as a pilot. Flying as in personally moving around at will in three dimensions.

Flying into formation. Front to back: Pat Melroy, Ron Luginbill, Matt Farmer, Jim Captain. Photographer Ray Cottingham

True when skydiving, everyone is falling earthward at the terminal velocity of about 120 mph, but it's all relative. If you decrease your speed by increasing your air resistance (extend arms and legs), you go up relative to others. Decrease your air resistance, and you go down. Stand on your head with legs together and arms tight along your side and you go down very fast, about 200 mph.

Going 200 mph gives you the ability to catch-up with skydivers who are far away. It also gives you a closing speed of 80 mph, plenty fast enough to hurt yourself or others, if you hit them while diving — which goes a long way toward explaining why freefall relative work became a brotherhood of young people with good eyes, quick minds and excellent reflexes.

At first skydivers were content to just see and maneuver relative to each other in freefall (i.e., flyby). Soon batons were being passed from one skydiver to another. Passing batons in freefall was a silly game, but it promoted skills needed to catch up with and fly close to others. Somewhere (exactly where is lost to history), a skydiver caught up to another skydiver in freefall, matched rates of fall, and they fell together hooked up hand to wrist. This simple "hookup" became the "base" for all star-building.

Near Seattle, in the mid '60's, a third skydiver caught up with and joined two others already hooked up. They all fell together in a formation. From then on, such circular formations were called "stars."

After three, any number of relative workers could enter the star without it losing the circular shape.

Entering a star required flying into a "slot" between two people already "in" the star and taking a grip on their arms in such a way that when they released their grip on each other, the star would increase by one and you would be "in."

During the early days of relative work, stars tended to slide and spin around the sky. As you can imagine, sliding and spinning made stars difficult to catch and join.

All Girl Record Star 1972, Zephyrhills, FL. Robbie Skinner, Nancy Guttman-Tyler, Pat Davis, Jeanne McCombes, Linda Heath, Chrissie Shinn, Donna Wardean Dann, Nancy Mills, Laurie Durava, Sylvia Lindgren, Patty Wilson. Photo by Ray Cottingham

Nevertheless, stars got bigger and bigger. The biggest star a skydiver had been in became a badge of honor. The first award for star size participation was created by Bill Newell in 1967 to honor Bob Buquor, a skydiver who died while filming a star attempt. The Bob Buquor Star Crest Memorial (SCR) indicated that the recipient had been in an eight-man or greater star. The actual award was a patch that could be sewn onto a jumpsuit or parachute pack for all to see. The skydiving SCRs were recorded and numbered according to date of application, much like sport parachuting licenses. Sport parachuting licensing was the domain of the Parachute Club of America (now the United States Parachute Association or USPA), and licenses were numbered according to date of application. There were four licenses, A, B, C and D, corresponding to increasing experience and presumably competency. Consecutive numbering of SCRs allowed skydivers to make the same kind of pointless numerical comparisons as had been so tedious with sport parachutists and their license numbers (e.g., my license number is lower than yours so I'm better) — which just goes to show you can change the game but you can't take the people out of people.

The largest stars became state, national or even world records. Having been in such a record star was considered a real accomplishment. Things could and did get political. In Texas, for instance, guns were sometimes brandished before or after record star loads — a uniquely Texan way of protesting who was or wasn't on a load. Elsewhere, it was usually just bad vibes. Relative work in the U.S. became a small (few hundred) community of larger-than-life individuals where reputation was everything because it determined who got on which loads or which competition teams.

Rise of Speed Star Competition

During the 1960's, a few large skydiving drop zones were developed on the West Coast of the U.S. These skydiving drop zones used larger airplanes, most notably the Beech-18 or "Twin Beech."

The Twin Beech could carry ten jumpers. It was not, otherwise, a great jump plane. The exit door was tiny, allowing only bent-over single file exits that spread jumpers out, making relative work more difficult by increasing the initial distance between jumpers in freefall. It was the unfortunate door geometry of the Twin Beech, more than anything, that created the head-long 200 mph dive style of skydiving that dominated the sport early on. The Twin Beech was also difficult to land and takeoff in the hands of the unskilled (as the Homegrown were to find out), but it carried ten jumpers and was, for its size, relatively cheap.

Soon there was friendly competition among West Coast jumpers to see who could overcome the spread-out Beech exit and make the first ten-man star. A few of the West Coast drop zones, finding they could each get all ten jumpers in a star, proposed competing to see whose jumpers could build the fastest (the shortest time between the first man out the door of the plane and the last man in the star). As you can imagine, it was nearly all men in those days.

It is skydiver legend that the first such contest was the result of a drunken bet, which pretty much tells you the amount of thought that went into the creation of speed star competition.

In the rest of the country and world, ten place jump planes were not common nor were ten-man stars. This set up an immediate disconnect between skydiving as practiced on most drop zones and skydiver competition. The officially recognized form of skydiver competition became the ten-man "speed star," yet most drop zones still had only four place jump planes.

Aircraft availability made skydiving competition the province and practice of a handful of California skydivers on a few large West Coast drop zones. To be sure, skydivers elsewhere could and did sometimes scrape up a Beech or other large airplane and ten skydivers to fill it. It's just that they could rarely do it often enough to be competitive. In California, skydivers on large drop zones jumped Twin Beeches every weekend and soon made ten-man speed stars as their primary focus. The focus on speed created a go fast, hit 'em hard, rock'em-sock'em relative work culture. The whole speed star thing was conceived and fueled by what my friend Skratch would call "testosterone poisoning."

Kamikazes

With closing speeds approaching 80 mph, people really felt strongly about who they did relative work with. Two hundred mph out-of-control "kamikaze" passes at stars or formations were strongly discouraged but not unusual in the early-days of relative work. It is a lot easier to dive at a target in freefall than it is to pull out of the dive, match speed with the target and then smoothly hook up with it.

Doc (Kent Farney) got caught-up in the all too serious consequences of a kamikaze pass at a star over a drop zone in Texas. Since most skydivers in Texas serious about relative work jumped at Valley Mills, this other Texas drop zone had trouble getting together a full Beech load of good skydivers. As a result, Doc ended up on a load with some questionable divers.

Doc was in and settling down to flying a nice star when a kamikaze roared in and landed right on the back of a guy across the star from Doc. The kamikaze hit so hard that the star was tipped up on edge. Because skydivers create violent air turbulences (called "burbles") above them as they fall, a star cannot fall on its edge. The high edge will "lose their air," tumble down and land on the low edge in what is called a funnel. People end-up bouncing off of each other and there is general mayhem for a couple of seconds until people can find some clean air again, get stable and get out of there.

Funnels are not just ugly and disorienting; they are dangerous. People get smacked around, lips get split and noses bloodied, though generally, jumpers are protected from serious injury by their helmets and parachute packs. The more serious danger is that a ripcord will accidentally get pulled and a parachute will get loose in the middle of the funnel. Once loose, the chute will do what it was designed to do: it will open and immediately slow its owner from 120 mph to 12 mph. Of course, everyone else caught in the funnel is still going 120 mph. That sets up the potential for collisions that can result in injuries far more serious than a split lip.

In this case, the kamikaze's reserve parachute opened in the middle of the funnel. Doc, among others, went right through the open canopy basically tearing it to shreds. Doc burned grooves in his arms and face as he was funneled down parachute lines toward the kamikaze dangling under his open, but badly damaged reserve. Doc acknowledges that the only reason he wasn't killed is that he didn't lose consciousness when he hit the kamikaze and was able get clear and open his own chute. He tells it as if it were a matter of good fortune, but my guess (knowing the Mad Doctor) is that he was sucking up the incredible pain being inflicted by those parachute line burns in order to stay conscious and best position himself for the inevitable impact so he'd have a chance to open his own parachute once clear. Like I said, quick minds and fast reflexes. Unfortunately, when it was all over, there was not enough left of the kamikaze's parachute to save him. A sad example of the serious nature of freefall relative work in the early days of skydiving. Skydivers got killed at the rate of about a hundred a year in those early days of skydiving. Not shocking given the total number of jumps made in a year, but enough to get your attention.

Skydiving Goes Its Own Way

The rise of skydiving and development of relative work as its object came with great cultural turmoil in the parachute world and no little anxiety on the part of the self-styled "founders" of sport parachuting. Sport parachutists had long competed in regimented style and accuracy events as individuals, jumping alone one at a time. For skydivers, relative work opened a whole new world of collective creativity and imagination.

Skydiving and sport parachuting began to diverge. Skydivers mostly came from the 1970's counterculture and carried with them that community's ambivalence for rules and authority. Sport parachutists, on the other hand, identified with the paratrooper roots of rule-bound, regimented parachute jumping. Skydivers favored long hair, bright multi-colored jumpsuits and wore lightweight tennis shoes. Parachutists often sported crewcuts, wore tight black jumpsuits and big, heavy, French paratrooper boots, making the two groups easy to tell apart.

The speed star culture spread until skydiving was almost entirely about big stars and fast stars. It was all about metrics for a while, but out on those small rural airstrips, bands of skydivers continued to pursue relative work for the beauty of the experience. It was their goal to fly smoother and prettier, not faster. It was the Homegrown's good fortune to become such a band in Kansas in the waning years of the 1960s.

There can be no better example of the increasing distance between skydivers and sport parachutists than Bob's description of his arrival at the 1970 National Collegiate Sport Parachute Championships in Deland, Florida (Nov. 22-28, 1970):

Our arrival was memorable. It was a long flight in the Doc's 182, but finally, we were circling the Deland airport. Dave McFadden and I put on our parachute rigs and asked Doc to give us some altitude. Why waste the chance for a free skydive, right? There were lots of typical Florida puffy cumulus clouds floating around, but occasional patches of blue sky. Dave and I wedged open the door and away we went. We hooked up, tracked and opened without thinking anything about it.

The spot turned out to be good in spite of the clouds. We were both able to land on the lawn in front of a building that looked like it was the center of the activity for the upcoming national parachute meet.

I was nonchalantly daisy-chaining my lines when a pack of three or four crew-cut dudes came boiling out of the building straight for us. The first words out of the leader's mouth were "You guys are grounded!!"

My involuntary response was "For what?"

"Cloud-busting is against the rules, and then there's the matter of your low pulls," their spokesman replied.

I, of course, had no idea what the hell he was talking about and I started to protest. He said if we wanted to appeal, we could appear before the USPA Board of Directors that was meeting that evening. I didn't know until the meeting that night that the spokesman earlier that day was none other than Jerry Rouillard, the USPA president. To make matters worse, he was the Head of the Board and conducting the hearing.

After hearing the official announcement of our infractions read out loud, he asked, "How do you plead?"

I replied, "Ignorant."

There was some spontaneous laughing, and I continued to explain that we had flown all the way from Kansas to compete, representing our college for the first time. I added that I had a newly acquired A license, 70 jumps and had no idea there was a cloud rule. I had never heard anyone at Sky High (my home drop zone) express any concern about clouds other than their effect on spotting. I think I added that where we came from, 1500-2000 ft was certainly not considered a low pull.

There was more laughing, and at that point, I basically threw myself and Dave on the mercy of the court. They huddled briefly and announced that we would be allowed to compete with the understanding that we would read the USPA procedure manual and agree to comply with every single regulation. We readily agreed and disaster was averted. The school newspaper had made a big deal out of our participation in a National Championship, and I was relieved to not have to think up some kind of excuse for how we got disqualified as soon as our feet hit the ground.

— Bob Johnson

PART 1

TRAJECTORIES

MATT FARMER

My skydiving career was mostly an extension of small drop zone parachuting, so I was never much caught up in the speed star craze. I learned and made my first 100 or so jumps with the Saigon Sport Parachute Club in Vietnam during 1966-67. The Saigon Sport Parachute Club was one of the thousands of sport parachute clubs organized all over the world after WWII.

Sport parachuting in a war zone was odd to say the least. Jumps were made from an old ARVN (Army of the Republic of Viet Nam) CH 34 helicopter flown by Vietnamese pilots we bribed with Johnny Walker whiskey and American cigarettes. The drop zone was a long abandoned Japanese supply compound left over from the Japanese conquest of Southeast Asia prior to WWII.

Matt under his 5-TU canopy, circa 1970.
Photographer unknown

At the time, sport parachutes were surplus military 28' round parachutes of the kind used by military pilots. For sport parachuting, the parachute was modified by cutting large openings in the rear of the chute to spill some of the air during descent. The escaping air gave the chute a small forward speed. Steering lines were attached to the openings, allowing the jumper to turn the chute right and left and thus to face upwind or downwind or crosswind. This small amount of control allowed the sufficiently skilled jumper to control, within limits, where and how they landed.

The Japanese compound serving as our drop zone in Vietnam was enclosed by tall fences topped with barbed wire. The jungle beyond the wire belonged to Charlie (enemy Vietnamese insurgents). This encouraged Saigon Parachute Club students to quickly learn parachute control. Not that there was a textbook or anything. You just watched and talked to the more experienced jumpers and tried to understand how it worked. Every jump in Vietnam was a chance to test your growing understanding of parachute control under the threat of enemy capture.

The guys who ran the show at the Saigon Sport Parachute Club gave students who showed promise (quick mind, sure hands, calm demeanor) a chance to learn more advanced aspects of sport parachuting, like spotting (directing the aircraft to the desired jump point upwind of the desired landing point) and putting out students (called being the "jumpmaster"). Other than spotting, being a jumpmaster mostly involved hooking up student static lines (the steady, sure hands part) and then getting the students to jump without resorting to violence (the calm demeanor part). I got to spot and jumpmaster a number of times in Vietnam.

While learning sport parachuting in Vietnam, I read an article in *Parachutist* magazine about the first three-man star near Seattle. I found the idea of chasing other jumpers in freefall and "hooking up" with them very exciting. I had seen other jumpers in freefall, but never tried to catch them. I read and reread the article, sat on my bunk, looked at the pictures and imagined what it would be like to fly like the guys in the *Parachutist* article.

Unfortunately for me, freefall relative work was unknown in Southeast Asia at the time. In fact, it was against club rules. Relative work was actively discouraged by most club members because of concerns about hitting someone in freefall or opening too close to each other or getting carried away and opening too low. I thought these concerns overblown. To my mind, such things, though dangerous, were not difficult to avoid and were minor considerations compared to the joys of freefall relative work.

Even though the club frowned on relative work, I started to look for someone in the Saigon club doing 30 second delays to chase and catch. I found a young Australian mercenary named Wally Morris willing to try and we spent many happy 30 second delays chasing each other around the Vietnamese sky. I would exit after him as closely as the jumpmaster would allow (not very close; after all what we were doing was against the rules). As soon as I was out, I would locate him and start doing whatever I could think of to get down to him. Mostly that involved flopping around like a fish. It was a steep learning curve, but I finally caught him. I still remember looking across at him as we fell together toward the abandoned Japanese compound carved out of the jungle far below. It was heady stuff for a hundred-jump wonder far-far from home.

Jumpmaster and International Sport Parachutist

When my year in Saigon was up, I put my chutes in my parachute bag and flew home to Minnesota where my parents picked me up. It was 1967. I was 19 years old and had just over a hundred jumps. On the ride home, I mentioned having taken up sport parachuting.

They told me there were people doing that at a local airport, and we decided to stop by on the way home. When we arrived, there was nothing there but a tumbled-down hangar and an old Cessna 182 with the right door missing. As I was getting out my parachute bag, the drop zone operator came over and asked if I wanted to make some jumps. I told him all my jumps were out of a big helicopter in Saigon, and I knew nothing about jumping out of a Cessna. He wanted to see my parachute jump log book and absently flipped through the pages until he got to the jumps where I was putting out static line students. There he stuck a finger in the book to hold his place and asked me if I wanted some free jumps.

All my jumps up until then had been essentially free, so I really didn't know what to say. Anyway, he soon had me in my jumpsuit and gear in the doorless 182 on my knees with my back to the instrument panel. He asked if I thought I could spot from that position, then clambered in on his knees in front of me and said, "I'm in the static line student's position. This ring right here by the door is the static line anchor point. You know how to hook up a static line, don't you?"

"Sure, sure, no sweat."

With that, he climbed out and returned a minute or two later with a gawky and geeky young hayseed wearing a static line parachute, a pair of old coveralls and a football helmet. Introductions were made. The kid climbed in on his knees in front of me and handed me the hook end of his static line. The drop zone operator walked around to the pilot's door, climbed in and said, "I don't suppose you 'cut' a helicopter for jumpers?"

I had no idea what he was talking about so I just said, "What's a cut?"

A "cut," he kindly told me, "Is when the pilot pulls the throttle back to idle to reduce the slipstream and make it easier for jumpers to climb out. You signal a cut to the pilot by drawing the edge of your hand across your throat, or yelling 'CUT' right before the jumpers get out. OK, you ready?"

I mustered all the parachutist bravado I was capable of at 100 jumps and told him, "Let's go."

Away we went, bouncing out to the grass runway. All was routine for takeoff, and soon we were up and turning onto a jump run at 3000 feet of altitude. I put a hand out on the wing strut, peered around the edge of the door frame and started giving the pilot 5-right and 5-left hand signals to guide him over the spot. I thought the hand signals more dignified than yelling five-right and five-left at him like an idiot. It was a mercy to discover that spotting hand signals are evidently universal.

Soon it was time for the main event. I hooked the student's static line to the ring, checked it several times, took another look out the door, swung back in and drew my hand across my throat.

The pilot quickly pulled back on the throttle; the engine sputtered twice and died. It was suddenly very quiet in that 182. As we glided on toward the spot, I turned to the student and using my very calmest demeanor, invited him to climb out on the step. To my surprise, he grabbed the wing strut and swung right out, but then fell off the step backward. I watched his chute open between his kicking feet; then I hopped out and pulled. Just like that, I was a Cessna jumpmaster and international sport parachutist.

Sky Ranch

Later that year, I moved to Topeka, Kansas in preparation for going to the University of Kansas (KU) in nearby Lawrence. Once settled, I began looking for a drop zone. It wasn't long before I found Sky Ranch. The place was a grass strip near Topeka with a few planes parked around a couple of T-hangars. One Cessna, a 180, had no right door or seat. Clearly, I had come to the right place.

Sky Ranch was run by Dick Hall, an Air Force Forward Combat Controller stationed at Forbes Field in Topeka. Air Force Forward Combat Controllers made up a significant part of the Saigon Sport Parachute Club. They were among the most experienced jumpers in the club and always willing to help a student.

I felt right at home on Dick's drop zone and jumped as much as I could afford. To afford more, I started putting out students for Dick. I had plenty of chances to practice my calm demeanor. In Dick, I found a mentor and role model. I wanted to have the same cool confidence as a jumper that Dick had.

I got to do a lot more relative work at Sky Ranch. A typical weekend load would be a static line student to get out at 3000', then any freefalling students to get out at the altitude appropriate to their opening delay and finally, one or two experienced jumpers doing 30 second delays from 7,500'. I'd play jumpmaster, getting the students out safely at the right altitudes, and then follow the experienced jumpers out for a little relative work — or baton passes or whatever kind of freefall grab-ass they were into in those days. It could be anything from throwing hedge apples at each other to picture-taking with an Instamatic to flying through hula hoops. It wasn't smooth or pretty but it was certainly a workout.

Stars were rare. Opportunities to interact with others in freefall were many. I got in my first three-man star at Sky Ranch. It was magical flying with a hookup and then swooping in to make it a star. I knew right then I was going to do a lot more of that sort of thing.

After a couple of years of this and another couple of hundred jumps, Dick died of a heart attack. He had been called to duty for another tour to Vietnam and collapsed while waiting to board the plane at Travis AFB. He was 33 years old. That was the end of Sky Ranch, not to mention the loss of my mentor, friend and role model.

Desoto, Kansas

With the loss of Sky Ranch, I was back to looking for a drop zone. The only drop zone I knew of at the time was on a farm near the little town of Desoto, Kansas between Lawrence and Kansas City. It was run, if that's the right word, by Jim Garrison (J.G.). J.G. was a Kansas City fireman, old-time sport parachutist, and absentee drop zone operator.

I had enough jumps by then to be considered very experienced and, once again, there was need of a competent jumpmaster. J.G. owned the jump plane and flew it. He paid for the plane and the pittance needed to rent the run-down farm by charging people, mostly KU college students, $35 to learn to jump. The drop zone was a business, if not a very lucrative one. I kept jumpmastering and then helping J.G. with the student instruction.

After a year or so, J.G. had a near death experience while jumping his Delta II "death wing." The parachute malfunctioned so severely while opening that it barely slowed him down. J.G. fiddled around with the malfunction trying to get it to open for so long (a few seconds) that he was at treetop level before he finally opened his reserve chute and saved his life. He was, quite literally, fractions of a second from dying.

J.G. disappeared more and more after that, until finally it was clear he was done with sport parachuting altogether. J.G.'s wife carried on for a while in J.G.'s stead, selling jumps and collecting from students. I handled the teaching and jumpmastering and organizing experienced jumpers into Cessna 180 loads.

After fumbling along like this for a while, J.G. showed up one weekend and offered to give me the drop zone if I'd pay for any flight time on the 180 and cover the rent on the farm. Just like that, I had a drop zone of my own.

While all this was going on, I'd been going to school at KU, letting my hair grow, and hanging out with the local chapter of the Vietnam Veterans Against the War and their hippie friends in Lawrence. Being a KU student myself, I could easily and effectively advertise "Make your first jump" to KU students.

I moved into the old farmhouse at the drop zone. It soon

became a hippie commune. We had a resident artist (Merv) and a rock and roll band that practiced in the barn. I enjoyed the weird lifestyle and loved having my own drop zone on which freefall relative work was the primary, indeed sacred, activity.

What I didn't have was a pilot. Then one day, out of the blue, a young sandy-haired Vietnam Vet with a laid- back attitude and a taste for good weed, named Herb Conley, walked on the drop zone and announced he was a newly minted commercial pilot who wondered if he might be able get some free pilot hours flying jumpers. A deal was quickly struck.

Herb moved into the farmhouse and became our resident 180 pilot. I taught Herb to skydive. He progressed rapidly and was soon doing smooth and pretty relative work with us every chance he got. To get more chances to skydive, Herb taught me to fly the 180.

I continued to teach KU students to jump to help make ends meet, and I carefully evaluated them for any potential

Matt Farmer and Herb Conley; Pat Melroy behind, circa 1970.   Photographer unknown.

to become relative workers. Pat Melroy, a jumper from the J.G. era, returned from two years in the Army and started to learn relative work at Sky High. Pat was an erudite small-town Kansan who jumped with us for years and was involved with us at The Gulch (Casa Grande, AZ) in pioneering formation skydiving and sequential relative work.

Another experienced jumper who was often around in the early days at Desoto was Harry Shill. Harry was a professional rodeo cowboy with the scars and belt buckles to prove it. Harry was a fearless and competent skydiver. We often counted on Harry to fill out loads. Harry, for instance, agreed to wedge himself in the 4-place 180 together with four other Homegrown when the Homegrown first started getting serious about relative work. In this way, we could do state record 5-man stars from a four-place airplane.

Kent (the Mad Doctor) Farney and "Ernie Bob" Johnson were among the first of the experienced jumpers who showed up at Desoto. Bob turned out to be a "twin brother from a different mother" and we have remained life-long friends. Doc and Ernie Bob were obvious kindred spirits; both stayed and became first-rate relative workers.

"B.A.", a downstate diver, talented fast hand and eye gamer, tribal healer and resident comedian came to fly with the Homegrown and stayed on to become a fine relative worker. Years later, he would visit us at The Gulch (Casa Grande, AZ) and take a position flying in the skydiving movie *Wings* even though the sequences being filmed were complicated and difficult, and everything, including mistakes, would be on film for every skydiver in the world to see. Heavy pressure — something B.A. thrived on.

Jim Baker, a "freak brother" Kansas City teenager learned to jump on a drop zone in central Kansas, but found Desoto once his interest turned to skydiving and relative work. Jim fit right in and was a true Homegrown in no time. He and I shared a love of wilderness adventure. We survived several such adventures together where the issue of survival was seriously in doubt.

The brightest of first jump students I trained during this period, was Jim Captain, another Kansas City teenager, and best natural skydiver I'd seen. Jim and I jumped together for years, became good friends and shared closely the development of sequential relative work and the smooth and pretty flying ethic.

Getting stoned with the anti-war people and talking relative work became the evening entertainment at the farm after a full day of packing parachutes, putting out students and doing better and better relative work. Initially nobody knew much more about relative work than I had when I started chasing Wally in Vietnam. You never really knew what you were going to see when you went out the door of the 180 in those earliest days of becoming skydivers. The joke was that mostly you'd just

Sky High, Circa 1971. L to R: Jan ,**, Jim Captain,**, Kent Farney, Mia Farmer, Boyd Mastin, Mel Carelli. Kneeling: **, Terry Toller, Matt Farmer, Harry Shill. Herb Conley in plane.
Photographer Boyd Mastin

see asses and elbows.

It wasn't long before a hard core of developing young relative workers began hanging out at the farm. We renamed the farm: "Sky High Skydivers." The core of freefall relative workers later became known as the "Kansas Homegrown," named after the killer pot we grew in the garden along with the rest of the staples common to a 1970's hippie commune. Despite our name and the circumstances, we were so serious about relative work that we adopted a strict policy against jumping stoned. They don't call it "dope" for nothing we'd tell each other.

As our skydiving skills grew and we had more and more adventures together, both in the air and on the ground, we began to develop a strong group identity. We were becoming a small tribe of freefall relative workers with a solid cohesive core.

A good on-the-ground example of Homegrown cohesion was the summertime money-making hybrid corn de-tasseling work we undertook as a group. To make hybrid corn, two different varieties of corn are planted in adjoining rows. It is then necessary to pull the tassels from one variety to make sure it is pollinated only by the other variety. To get this done, the seed corn companies contract with local groups to walk the corn rows and pull out the unwanted tassels. The pay per acre was based on the companies' experience with local productivity. The work was so unpleasant and physically demanding, that companies found they could keep crews in the field only by paying dearly per acre of de-tasseled corn.

Our group cohesiveness, ability to function as a unit at full potential without regard to negative environmental stimuli, and, of course, those same sure, steady hands allowed us to pull tassels way more quickly and, therefore, make a lot more money than other contractors. In this way, we could all stash away funds during the summer to get ready for fall and winter skydiving season in Texas, Florida and Arizona.

A good example of in-the-air adventures was the series of rodeo demonstration jumps we undertook. We made the first rodeo arena jump near Kansas City. We did a 4-way star overhead and got a tight opening "stack" (the relative positions of the parachutes after opening). Because we all jumped "rags" (5-TU round parachutes), our descent rates under parachute were about the same. The tight stack allowed us to land one right after the other in the small arena much to the pleasure and excitement of the rodeo spectators. The promoters were greatly pleased, and more rodeo demonstration jumps around Kansas and Missouri followed.

These jumps helped forge the Homegrown into serious skydivers. We became much more aware of each other and how we interacted under stress.

Packed into the 180 together and flying cross country trying to find a small rodeo arena, then climbing up to 7500' to put on a skydiving demonstration jump is stressful. It is actually a relief when the jump-door is finally opened, the engine cut and guys begin climbing out.

At that point, the wait is over. It's happening. You climb out on the step and peer down trying to find that little arena you're going to land in a mile and a half below somewhere in the unfamiliar countryside slipping slowly beneath the 180's nose. Now is the time for sure steady hands, close coordination, and a very calm demeanor.

First comes the exit. A simultaneous departure is critical and requires concentration, close coordination, and no mistakes. Next comes the relative work and building the star. Although it is always the most fun, it is also stressful because everyone must get in and you have to do it fast so there will be plenty of time to hold the star for the crowd to see. Looking around the star at your friends as you all streak through 3000', you know that each one is, like you, making a careful calculation about when to let go, separate and pull his ripcord. You have to get everything right to avoid a dangerous canopy entanglement and still have the tight stack you need for the demo. That requires real faith in each other.

Once everyone is under open canopies comes the really hard part — maneuvering your beat-up old rag of a parachute in high winds to land in that small dirt arena. This takes as much, if not more, daring as skill. And it requires a lot of skill. Such jumps are true exercises in keeping the faith in yourself and each other. You need to be able to look into the faces of the other jumpers and see they are right there with you and not off somewhere struggling with their own doubts or demons. If you look and see calm confident faces looking back, you've found your solid cohesive core.

Beyond daring demo jumps, we all wanted to do something more with our growing relative work skills. There were problems: (1) none of us (other than me) had ever jumped from anything other than a small light plane like our 180; (2) none of us had yet been in anything nearly as big as a 10-man star.

We thought to remedy all this by getting together with the sport parachute club at the nearby small town of Edgerton to see if we might be able to fly our two small planes in formation to get us in the air together with a plane full of their best skydivers. This wouldn't get us ten, but eight was a start. As a bonus, airplane formation jumps are always visually spectacular, and it is great fun to chase jumpers exiting from a different plane (talk about spread out).

We did finally get the two planes together, and things went well enough to break the existing state star record of five. Although the founders and operators of the Edgerton club remained suspicious of us and our (rumored) freakish ways, their small relative work core, the "Edgerton Boys," (Ken Kenable, Rick Bridges, John Massey) warmed to us sufficiently that we could jump with them when the chance arose.

26

With them on board and a few regular Sky High visitors like C Pigg and Jim Borovicka or Tommy Bullion, we thought we could turn out ten relative workers. We went looking for a Twin Beech we might rent. That effort ended in an infamous (front page of the *Kansas City Star*) fiery crash and destruction of the Beech, but no loss of life or injury. Here's the story:

"Beech Burn"   May 20, 1972

If you want to talk about the Kansas Homegrown Beech crash back in 1972, you have to talk about Ted, the wanna-be Beech-driver. Ted was one of those clean-shaven, crew-cut losers left over from the 1950's that you sometimes ran into around aviation all the way into the 1970's. We met Ted through Walt, a nice old man who bought a Twin Beech from the government for pennies on the dollar right after WWII. He kept it maintained and flying but by the time we got word of a ten-place airplane in our area, the operating expense was killing him, so when a bunch of skydivers tracked him down and offered to "rent" the plane, greed got the better of him.

Walt soon found himself at the controls of his over-loaded Twin Beech flying a boring "best rate of climb" run to "10-5." At that altitude, his passengers began to gather around the little open door at the back of the plane. One of them kneeled in the open door, looked out and started waving a hand back and forth. Soon they all started yelling "5-left" and "5-right," often, it seemed to Walt, at the same time. The next thing you know the kneeler crawled back in, stood-up, and started yelling," Cut! Cut! cut!" in a hysterical tone.

As soon as Walt throttled back the engines, three of the passengers climbed out the little door and hung on the outside of the airplane. The rest lined up single-file at the door. After a few seconds someone yelled "GO" at the top of his lungs, and they all dove out the little door headfirst and disappeared into

27

the slipstream.

The skydiving apparently over, Walt began the long slow descent back to the airport. We later figured it was during this long descent that Walt began racking his brain for another pilot who might be willing to fly these skydivers with his Twin Beech. Evidently, "TED" was the name that came to his mind.

The very next weekend, we found ourselves packed in Walt's Twin Beech with Ted's pink-faced crew-cut head peering around the edge of the coffin-shaped cockpit door and Walt on his right. It was only much later that we learned Ted had no tail-dragger time (piloting experience in a plane with 2 large wheels forward of the plane's center of gravity and a small wheel or skid under the tail) and no time flying a Twin Beech whatsoever.

Those of you with any knowledge of tail-draggers and Twin Beeches probably are, like us at the time, wondering if there was any way in hell Ted could get that plane off the ground. As it turned out, there was. In fact, he got it off the ground six times on the first takeoff run alone. On the sixth bounce, he was able to stagger into the air and jerk the gear up before she stalled. That lucky bounce allowed Ted to roar off at full-throttle six feet above the Kansas plain. Ted had his first Beech takeoff under his belt.

The only reason he got six tries at this style of takeoff was that he usually wasn't quick enough to get the gear up before she stalled back on and took another bounce. That Ted kept from ground-looping (uncontrollably spinning the plane while still in ground contact causing a wing to dip and strike the ground) that first day was nothing but the good luck of having Walt in the right seat. Luck that, as it turned out, was only good for that first day.

With hindsight, it is easy to see that we were crazy to ever get back in that plane with Ted. But we were young relative workers; it was the 1970's; and Ted came with the only ten-place airplane available. So, it wasn't really even a close call.

The next weekend Walt rode shotgun with Ted again. We got a few jumps in before Walt got bored and went home, which brings us at long last, to the "Beech Burn" itself and the less than somber picture-taking that followed.

On his next takeoff attempt Ted only got three bounces. On the third bounce, he stalled back on the runway so hard going sideways, that the right landing gear collapsed completely. This bent the right wing up at a hideous angle and allowed the right engine to slam directly into the pavement, running at takeoff power. The impact was so violent the engine was torn completely out of the wing and began bouncing along behind us as we spun helplessly along the runway in a great shower of sparks and little pieces of Twin Beech. This sad state of affairs continued the length of the runway, rearranging the stunned skydivers inside several times as it went. Mercifully, when the Beech hit the grass at the end of the runway, it stopped spinning and began to slow as it dug a tattered ditch toward the highway.

When the motion finally stopped, our burly base guys were all in a pile against the rear bulkhead. Doc Farney (the Mad Doctor), who had been positioned in the middle of the load, found himself comfortably seated right at the open exit door. With no landing gear, the ground was only six inches down. The Doc, being a man of iron nerve, simply stepped out and walked off, shaking his head.

I was not so lucky. The only thing the bounces and spins did for me was deposit two more skinny "flyers" on top of me in the right front corner of the cabin. While we sorted this out, we all began seriously eyeing that little (it looked about the size of a toilet seat to us) open door at the back of the plane.

Ted stuck his head into the cabin with the helpful hint that we should "GET OUT." This, not surprisingly given

Ted's standing with us at the time, had no effect whatsoever. Seconds later, however, Tom Bullion, the skydiver riding up-front with Ted, stuck head and shoulders into the cabin, yelled "FIRE" in a loud clear voice, then tripped on his way out of the cockpit and landed on the pile on top of me. The effect of the word "FIRE" was immediate (except for me, of course): instantly there was an orderly line at the door and a record fast exit — no doubt accelerated by the now visible flames dancing all along the right wing and beginning to lap at the fuselage.

By the time everyone was out, the avgas-fueled fire was shooting twenty feet in the air. This evidently attracted the attention of local authorities. No sooner was I out, than up the road from town, sirens blaring and lights flashing, came the local volunteer fire department.

Three brave volunteers rode in full gear on back of the truck, ready (literally, as it turned out) to jump into action. Up the road and through the airport gates they came at a blistering pace, past the T-hangars and right up to the burning Beech. There they came to a rolling stop, and the three volunteers on the back jumped off, hoses in hand. No sooner had their feet hit the grass than the now half-empty fuel tank in the right wing exploded with a roar, shooting fire, ash and debris fifty feet in the air.

The volunteers jumped back on the truck. The truck did a fast U-turn, sped back past the T-hangars, out the airport gate, and disappeared down the road toward town. The Beech sat there and burned. We stood around joking and savoring the sweet feel of life. Grinning Team pictures followed.

Soon it became clear our presence was no longer required. The "Team", therefore, loaded up and retired to the top of a nearby hill where we sat in the grass in a circle and looked out over at the airport with the still burning Beech smoking away at the end of the runway. "Jacque Le Bong", the Homegrown's only real asset, was soon loaded with the Team's namesake weed and passed around the circle.

Those who have met Le Bong can easily understand what happened next. Having met Jacque or not, old school skydivers will have no trouble conjuring an image. No one knows how many times Le Bong's bowl was filled that afternoon because after the first few refills, the hill ceased to exist in a dimension where there were such things as "numbers" and "counting."

Finally, as was not infrequently the case when "Homegrown" teamed with Le Bong, the whole thing broke up when the dimension that included activities like "loading," "lighting," and "passing" slipped away. Then there were just ten guys sitting on top of a hill somewhere in Kansas.

It was a mediocre ten-man team that had climbed into the Beech that morning, but it was a determined band of skydiving

Beech Burn 1972. L to R Back: Jim Captain, Kent Farney, Matt Farmer, Tom Bullion, Mike Canella. Front: Harry Shill, C. Pigg, Jim Baker, "Boris" Borovicka.
Photographer Diane Bullion

brothers who came down the hill that afternoon. We felt like shiny translucent creatures of the sky who had, as John Lennon imagined, "No Hell below us. Above us only sky." All the while, the Beech burned quietly in the distance.

Beyond Kansas

Following the Beech Burn and our quasi-religious experience on the hill afterward, there were several suggestions for what to do with skydiving. One was that we all somehow get to Zephyrhills, Florida for the next "boogie" (skydiving meet) scheduled for November 1972. Another was to check out the Twin Beech that Doc and Ernie Bob had found in Valley Mills, Texas six months earlier (November, 1971). Both ideas were accepted. Texas was to come first so we could get some more Beech jumps before venturing to Z-Hills.

Before heading to Texas, we learned of a five-man meet in Oswego, Kansas. Of course, Oswego got added to the itinerary and turned out to be great fun. We pulled up at the drop zone in Captain's mother's big Oldsmobile convertible we called the "Belch-fire" because of its big V-8 engine and twin glass-pack mufflers. We unloaded our chutes and signed-up for the five-way speed-star contest.

The organizers said," Glad you're here — you guys are up."

We just pulled on our gear and climbed into their beautiful retractable gear Cessna-210. Within 10 minutes of arrival, we were stacked in the big door of that 210 at 7500' counting down the exit: "Ready. Ready. Go!"

What a great exit door on the 210, and the jump-run speed is fast enough that you can start doing relative work as soon as your butt clears the door frame. A few seconds later you've pretty much got a 5-way, and that's just what happened. We looked around the star at each other and nodded. That was the signal to drop grips, do a back-flip and then re-build the star. It was a routine we'd been working on ever since seeing the James Gang do it with a 10-way at Z-hills, FL.

We had the whole routine done by the time we reached break-off altitude at 3500', but Captain and B.A. weren't ready to quit. When we broke to open, they did another hook-up and kept right on falling, with the rest of us chasing them for a third 5-way. How low we went that day is a matter of conjecture and dispute. It was certainly low (not USPA low), scary low, and we knew it.

Needless to say, we got the attention of the meet organizers. As soon as we landed, they told us we had won the meet with the fastest star; then grounded us for pulling low and, given the flagrant nature of the violation, asked us to get back in the Belch-fire and go home.

We left, but not before we had a chance to meet and visit with Ron Luginbill, an old-time skydiver from Texas. Ron is a gentle giant with a wing-span well over six feet. That made him a great stable target from which to build formations, especially diamonds. [It also made him the perfect stunt-double for Jaws in the James Bond movies.] Ron told us there was good skydiving in the winter at Casa Grande, Arizona.

Then it was on to Valley Mills, Texas where we made many friends with Texas relative workers. Over the next year, the Homegrown tribe often traveled to Texas for large (up to 30) star attempts. Many attempts were, in the parlance of the day, "real cluster f--ks." Some, however, resulted in Texas records. In the process, we were learning about jumping with more people from larger planes. We were also starting to feel more strongly the siren song of the big West Coast drop zones.

Valley Mills TX skydivers, circa 1970s. L to R Standing: Phil Mayfield, Anita Howe, Sandy Roberts, John Mincher, Wayne Mosley, Phil Smith, Lyn Fitts (Mayfield), Autumne, Gregg Hackett, Bobby Brown. Kneeling: Bill Minyard,(Ed Westcott's girlfriend), Ed Westcott, Ken Gillespie.   Photographer unknown

Back to Kansas

Returning to Desoto, we found the 180 down with serious engine problems; so serious, its return was doubtful. To fill the gap, we found an old gull-wing Stinson V-77 to rent. It was an antique, fabric-covered plane with a large door but no jump step. To exit, one had the choice of hanging out the door, dangling from the wing strut, or climbing down the landing gear strut and diving off the wheel. Everybody seemed to have their own favorite, and Stinson exits soon started to look more like a barnstorming stunt than a skydiving exit.

The good times flowed once again at Desoto, until the guy we rented the Stinson from demanded it back. That put us back on the street, looking for a ride once again.

Invitation Only Drop Zone

In 1973, a beautiful five-place Cessna 205 with a willing owner was found at the Lawrence Municipal Airport. Big problems though: the pilot would not fly his plane off the short dirt strip at Sky High, and Lawrence Municipal was not off the beaten path. There was a lot of private aviation at Lawrence. For that reason, the airport officials wanted nothing to do with skydivers.

To allay their fears and objections, I was forced to explain that only the most experienced and serious of skydivers would be allowed to jump at Lawrence — no students, period. I ended up assuring the airport officials and the pilot that jumping at Lawrence would be by personal invitation only, and I would be responsible.

They bought it, and invitations were soon extended to the Homegrown and a few area jumpers known to be solvent, honest, able to do relative work, and skilled enough parachutists to not land on active runways, hangars or parked aircraft. I was taking a big risk setting up such a drop zone, but it couldn't have worked better.

No jump tickets were sold or manifests kept. The cost of a jump from 7500' was announced (there were no jumps from other altitudes), and at the end of the day, the pilot would sit at a table in the airport pilot's lounge and jumpers would file by and pay the pilot directly for the jumps they had made. All jump debts were promptly settled, and the pilot told us he'd be happy to fly us whenever we wanted.

There were no parachuting incidents or accidents at Lawrence. The atmosphere was one of dedication to the most progressive relative work and very best skydiving possible. We created and built a five-way formation we called a "spider." The spider was our first baby step away from stars. We didn't know it at the time, but being able to build a reliable spider proved very useful when we started building bigger formations and sequences of formations in Casa Grande the next winter.

We built those first spiders by building a three- way star and then opening it to a line to give us star-like "slots" to fly into, but it quickly proved a clumsy (and slow) way to start large diamonds and wedges. We had to give it up in favor of just flying to a skydiver's single limb in whatever orientation necessary for your position in the formation. If that meant flying sideways or even backward, so be it. Opening a star did, however, give us our first taste of "flying station" with a formation. "Flying station" means holding a steady position relative to a formation or another skydiver in freefall. It was something speed star people never did because they were always moving toward the star as fast as possible.

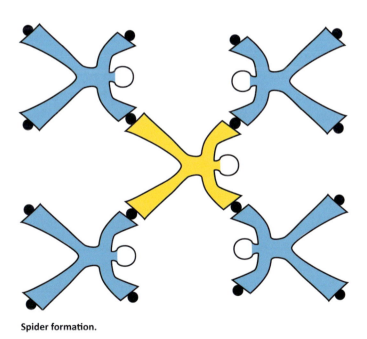

Spider formation.

Big Eat

One of the flights we wanted to do was a demonstration jump into the 1973 "Big Eat", an annual counter-culture "fair" of food and music, dope, beer and "good vibes" held in the country near Lawrence each summer. I was in a cast at the time with a broken ankle due to a work accident. I did aerial construction for a cable TV company and accidents were not uncommon. In order for me to participate, Jim Baker was kind enough to cut the cast off with a pair of rusty tin snips.

We built a pretty 5-way star right over the party and then landed among the revelers. On landing, Ernie Bob's chute was blown against one of the Harleys attending bikers had lined up in the clearing. The bikers felt their honor had been besmirched by the skydivers. It looked like it might come to blows or worse until Ernie Bob noticed a biker take a pull from his Jack Daniels bottle and asked for a shot.

After Bob, we each stepped up in turn and took a pull from the bottle. Soon the bikers gathered around and started asking about that circle they had seen us form in the sky and how we were all able to land one after another right at the party. Homegrown from our garden was rolled and passed. Everyone parted friends.

We enjoyed ourselves and got better for the rest of the summer. Once the cast was off my ankle, I found I could wear my heavy Vibram-soled hiking boots and walk just fine. With the workman's comp checks rolling in for six weeks, I decided it was a good time to spend a summer backpacking in the high mountains of Colorado while the ankle finished healing. That may sound crazy, but the alternative was to stick around and do half a dozen or so parachute landings a week on the partially healed ankle. I headed to Colorado. Everyone else continued to look for novel skydiving opportunities. One such opportunity was a Kansas record star attempt at Oswego.

Oswego Record Star

The Oswego divers were always looking for ways to keep their Cessna 210 busy. To that end, they put out the word in the local skydiving community that they would like to host an attempt at the Kansas record star which stood at 12. That meant they would need to come up with a big plane like a DC-3 or string together a formation of small planes such as never before seen in Kansas. Having no DC-3, they went for the formation.

The Homegrown lined up the Lawrence Cessna 205, the Oswego guys had their Cessna 210. Together the two planes would carry ten jumpers. They were three jumpers short of a new record. To make it work, a local Cessna 180 was pressed into service for the day of the attempts.

Ron Luginbill graciously offered to go base. Bridges offered to pin him (base and pin form the initial hookup from which a star builds). Luginbill and Bridges were to jump from the 210 along with three of Oswego's best. In this way, it was hoped

Record 13-man star, Oswego, KS 1972. L to R Back: Roger Massey, Bob Johnson, Rick Bridges, Jim Captain, Ken Knable. Kneeling: Pat Melroy, Jim Baker, Tom Bullion, JJ Johnson. Sitting: Al Hively,**,Kurt Yoakam, Ron Luginbill.   Photographer Larry Apt

that a quick solid 5-way could be built to give jumpers from the other planes something substantial to see and aim at. That's just how it went that day in Oswego.

A quick solid base-pin gave Oswego's best a chance to make it 5 before they even hit terminal velocity. The 8 jumpers straggling out of the other airplanes did have something to see and aim at. One by one they showed up and entered the star until there was a big round Kansas record star falling over the Oswego airport. There is no picture of the star, but there is one of the jumpers who built it.

A big part of getting better as skydivers that last summer in Kansas was understanding that a jumper's vertical velocity on exit is zero and accelerates very slowly at first then faster and faster until terminal velocity is reached some 12 seconds or so after exit. A jumper's horizontal velocity on exit, however, is the speed of the airplane (a hundred miles an hour or more) and then slows steadily.

True to Galileo's experiments, everyone accelerates earthward at the same rate once their inertia is overcome by gravity. We noticed this visually in small plane exits where all of us were off the plane at virtually the same time. Any small difference in leaving the plane would be expressed in horizontal separation, not vertical separation.

More importantly, the air resistance one had to work with in the first seconds of freefall was horizontal, not vertical. Slower exits meant greater horizontal separation, not (unless the exit is very long) vertical separation.

Bomb trajectory illustrating freefall arc.
Forum ww2aircraft.net

A skydiver's trajectory, like that of a bomb, is a long smooth arc that is as nearly horizontal initially as it is vertical ultimately. Consecutive jumpers, like a stick of bombs, scribe parallel trajectories separated horizontally by their drop interval with very little initial vertical separation.

What this meant was that the smoothest and prettiest way to do relative work was to use the initial seconds of freefall to move closer to each other, then let gravity accelerate everyone vertically to terminal velocity together. During this gravity fueled acceleration, there would be plenty of time (10 seconds or so) to move into position for the final smooth swoop and hook-up. As far as speed was concerned, we believed the fictitious seagull flyer, Jonathan Livingston Seagull, got the right advice when he was told, "Perfect speed is being there."

"Being there" has special meaning in smooth and pretty formation skydiving. Because formations build one person at a time in proper order, it is as bad to get to your position too early as too late. Ideally a formation will build at a smooth constant pace. Taking your assigned position right on that pace is "being there." Being there soon replaced speed as the most important skill a skydiver could acquire.

The Homegrown, being avid followers of Jonathan Livingston Seagull, had a good understanding of the importance of being there and often marveled that a skinny parable about a seagull could include such an important relative work insight. Richard Bach, the author of *Jonathan Livingston Seagull*, dropped by Lawrence in his bright red bi-plane one weekend that summer. We sat around behind a hangar, passed some "homegrown" and bent his ear about the spirituality and beauty involved in freefall relative work and thanked him for his wonderful parable about the joy of flying. Ernie Bob later got a postcard from him that Bob still has today, nearly fifty years later.

The Gulch

Come winter 1973, the Homegrown quit their day-jobs, loaded their junker cars with parachutes, and headed to Casa Grande, Arizona by way of Colorado and Elsinore, California. (Like I said, gas was cheap). My junker car, an early 1960's Chevy, was called "Hundred-dollar car" because that's what I paid for it. I traveled with a toolbox in the back seat and a case of cheap oil (and cheap beer) in the trunk. The car and passengers smoked all the way to Arizona. Passengers smoked homegrown; the car, cheap oil.

Casa Grande (aka The Gulch) was in the middle of the Arizona desert between Phoenix and Tucson. Twelve jumpers died at The Gulch the first year we were there. At times, jumping at The Gulch felt, to borrow a metaphor from The Eagles, like jumping on a drop zone full of "tombstones just waiting for the names." This gave The Gulch a weird (dangerous) reputation of a place suitable only for people willing to pursue relative work at any cost.

One of the twelve deaths was that of our friend and accomplished sky diver, Jim Heydorn. Here's the story I wrote about it at the time, taken from the *RWunderground Newsletter* (Pat Works, Editor), the only skydiver publication willing to print such a story:

This is going to be a good one. I can feel everyone psyching up for it, as we turn jump run. Quinn is up front, keeping everybody loose and the vibes up.

"Alright, let's do it!"

"Air dive, Air dive, feels great."

"Air dive, Air dive, can't wait."

The Twin Beech vibrates at a new pitch, as the driver throttles back. Floaters swing through the door and hang waiting. We move quickly to stack ourselves in the door.

Heydorn is in the door. I slide in behind and Luginbill leans tightly over the two of us. Melroy, Captain, Wooten, Herman and Gruber take their places.

Between Heydorn's back pack and the top of the door, I can see Chuck and Quinn watching me intently for the start of the count. Their jumpsuits are already flapping in the wind we will all feel in a second.

"Ready!"

Gruber starts the count.

"Ready." Comes back the response.

"Stacked in the door and counting, I can feel the adrenalin flow, mind and body winding up-

«Go!»

We explode from the tight confines of the Beech into a bright blue sky two miles deep and stretching from horizon to horizon.

I catch a good exit and look for Heydorn. He's right in position and the floaters are close behind him, tracking up on the still slow air. Quinn is up and on first with a beautiful fingertip dock. I close facing him on Heydorn's left hand. Chuck's up from the other float slot as Luginbill docks beside me on Heydorn's right arm. A five-spider fast, clean and stable.

Looking out for Melroy's side-in approach, I catch in my periphery above us Gruber's flare to the point of the rapidly building formation. He is perhaps fifteen feet above us, head down to the point of being nearly vertical, fully flared against the momentum of his aggressive approach speed. He looks like a flying squirrel in a desperate full spread flight to a small tree branch. Melroy slides into his side-in slot and Quinn and I catch him with no trouble. It's going great.

I glance over my shoulder to see where Wooten is. He's on a smooth final to the tip slot on Melroy's leg. Gruber's already in on the point and Captain has finished his side-in on the other side of the spider when I look back across the *now nearly complete ten-wedge. Only the two tips are out and they close a heartbeat later, right on the pace. Little more than 25 seconds have passed since exit, the base formation is complete.*

Everyone's attention is on Heydorn. He will key the break with a simple nod of his head. Ready — Now, he nods, hands release grips, the ten-wedge breaks into three pieces. Two three-man wedges separate from a four-man diamond. The two wedges are side by side, facing the diamond.

As the pieces begin to separate, the wedge that I am a wingman of turns a quick 180. The other wedge turns with us, between us and the diamond. Melroy, Wooten and I are the base wedge. We take up a heading, trying hard to hold it and fall straight down. I take a quick look over my inside shoulder and see the other wedge move into position behind us, ten feet up and ten feet out. The diamond is right behind them, on their level or maybe a little lower.

My gauge (altimeter) reads five grand. We've got the time. The three pieces are in position and we can dock them to triple diamonds (the second formation of the sequence), if we hurry. I take a glance at the ground, then back at the gauge. Coming up on four grand — still no dock. I look back over my shoulder again.

The other wedge is almost on us. They are shooting a very vertical approach, carrying a lot of speed. Captain on the point of their wedge has his arms back and up; Luginbill and Herman, his wingmen, are tucked up tight. The diamond is in close, already on our level, moving for the slot that will be there when the wedge docks.

Crash, the wedge, unable to brake all their vertical approach speed, comes on hard. Captain catches the grips and we struggle to regain stability. Before we can dampen the effects of the hard dock, the diamond, already committed, piles into the back of the two struggling wedges. Heydorn, on the point of the diamond, comes up with a grip on Luginbill. We fight for stability. The oscillation begins to dampen but the formation distorts where the grip is missing between Heydorn and Herman. Tension pulls at the formation; we struggle to stabilize and connect the open grip. It's no good — Snap, we lose the other grip. The formation starts to break up.

I let go, turn to my left and lay it back into a track. Right at three grand, safe and sane, I track hard, then sit up and look over my shoulder. Above and far off to my right, I see Heydorn unload his P.C Nothing over the other shoulder, I wave and punch. My rag comes off clean and I feel the steady pull of opening. Just as I'm getting the opening shock, I see Heydorn again, not a hundred feet away, still at terminal velocity. His P.C. is streamering (complete failure to open).

Words flash in my mind. Streamer ... Streamer ... cut-it-away ... cut it ... Long before the words can be verbalized, I see — seemingly in the very instant I perceive his situation — a flash of white, his reserve.

The scene screams away toward the earth. I watch. Stark white against the dark red and black of his tangled main, the reserve streams out. It doesn't bloom. It's tangled; tangled in the mess of line and canopy over his head.

Fear! Fear for this man, my friend. Fear born of knowledge. Knowledge of time and speed and the ground.

The words pour out.

"Come on ... Come on ... pull it out, pull it out."

Seconds tear by. I watch, far below, the ground, the still hurtling figure, the flapping tangle of red, black and white. I watch, small now against the enormous earth, the man and the flapping un-opening chutes.

Fear and helplessness — my thoughts race — the time — Christ, the time — come on — come on. I can see it's too late only an instant before he collides with the planet. A ring of dust and sand explodes outward from the violence of the *impact. The flapping tangle of nylon lies still against the hard brown desert.*

Dead. Oh, God. he's dead. Not five seconds have passed. Five seconds, a life time. I hang spent, drifting slowly toward the desert under my breathing canopy. A deep sadness washes over me. I feel empty.

On the ground I can see cars stopping on the highway. People are running from the hangars to form a small circle around the smashed, lifeless figure. I am momentarily angry at these vultures. What do they want here? Do they think they will understand something of their own impending deaths by staring blankly at this man's?

I land and walk toward the hangar. The spectators drifting past me look curiously at the parachute rolled in my arms, Their eyes are bright as they hurry to see violent death. They don't understand the loss. What can they know of Heydorn — of fast hands and a quick mind, of an easy laugh and his intense personal sanity. To them it is only an opportunity to see a newspaper headline in real life. — Chutist Falls — Something to tell at work Monday.

Those of us who were on the dive drift slowly into the packing area. Eyes sad, movements strangely slow and deliberate. No one quite knows what to do with themselves — I am here, but my friend is dead. We stand in a small circle around Ron's van. There are short snatches of conversation.

"It doesn't seem real — not somebody like Heydorn."
"A streamer."
"No cut-away."
«Entanglement.»
"Fought it all the way in."
"God, did you see him hit."

The conversation dies out, each of us lost in his own thoughts,

Thoughts about dying — about this odd chain of events we

call life that leads us to it. He made a mistake. You can dump a reserve past a streamer sometimes. — A chance. He rolled and lost. Now he's lying in a broken heap out by the highway and I'm sitting here feeling the hot sun on my back and wondering. Wondering what it is we seek in freefall. Why are we here?

"Hey, that was a good dive."

Someone breaks the silence.

"Yea, that spider was right there."

Someone else picks it up.

"Quick wedge."

"Really."

"That was a nice swoop, Grube."

"The break to pieces looked good to me."

"Yea, but, when the lead wedge turned, it dropped down and away."

"Right, and vertical separation makes it hard."

The conversation rambles on slowly. I'm half listening and thinking — Well, what are we doing? Our friend is dead and we are standing here talking over the dive. But we're skydivers and so was Heydorn. Our lives and perhaps our deaths are tied up in this thing we call skydiving. Who's to say? We are only human, so we all live to die — and there are many ways to die — many ways. You can be so afraid of dying that you can't live.

Life is what skydiving is all about. In free-fall you know you're alive. You're right there on the edge where the world is moving. Where time is right now. Jimmy Hendrix said it right —

"I'm the one who has to die when it's my time to go, so let me live my life the way I want to."

The talk is slowing down. I glance up, squinting against the setting sun to see who's talking. It's Luginbill, big hands thrust deep in his blue jean pockets, kicking aimlessly at the gravel with his toe and summing it up in one easy sentence-

"Yea, well, no sweat, we'll get it. All we need is a few more dives."

The Gulch was a large drop zone with a couple of Beech 18s and a much larger Lockheed Lodestar, a twenty-place old-time civilian airliner from the 1930's.

The drop zone was run by Mike Larson and his business partner, Bob Schaffer.

Pilot Randy Kempf and Mike Larson, pilot and owner of
The Gulch DZ.   Photo courtesy Mike Larson.

Mike was a brilliant drop zone operator who, in circumstances that would have crippled a lesser man, kept his fleet of large antique airplanes flying, and the freak show of 1970's relative workers they attracted from "going completely off the reservation."

At the same time he allowed the kind of open environment that fostered experimentation and excellence. If I had to pick the one person most responsible for the quantum leap the sport took from speed stars to formation skydiving in the early 1970s, I'd pick Mike Larson.

Typical 1970s freak show at The Gulch. L to R Standing: Chuck Wooten, Gary Hod Sanders, Pat Melroy, Dave Singer, Matt Farmer, Jim Captain, Ron Luginbill, Chirp Navrotski, Rande DeLuca. Kneeling: Ron Herman, Ed Dugan, Ruben Casarez, Steve Gras, Larry Duff, Ken Gruber Gorman, Ernie Stark, John Quinn,**.   Photographer unknown

Given its proximity to the West Coast, there were a few experienced speed star people around The Gulch, but that was not the culture of the drop zone by any means. Rather, Casa Grande was, in the early 1970's, a "small" drop zone with big airplanes. Because of the planes, there were more jumpers around than typical of a small drop zone, especially after the Homegrown showed up, but no dedicated competitive speed star teams.

Indeed, the only identifiable local clique of jumpers was the "whiskey divers," a group of old-time Phoenix skydivers who drank whiskey all day at the drop zone and made "fun jumps" (jumps with little or no specific plan — a throwback to sport parachuting days).

I had never seen whiskey consumed on a drop zone and hadn't seen "fun jumpers" since teaching myself relative work at Sky Ranch. We tended to avoid the whiskey divers and fell into the habit of jumping with each other and just a few new friends.

A very special friend we made at The Gulch was Ray Cottingham. Ray was widely considered the best freefall photographer in the world. I also thought Ray was one of the best skydivers I'd seen because he could not only precision skydive but take outstanding pictures as he performed within a formation or sequence.

Another photographer we immediately bonded with at The Gulch was Rande Deluca, whose day job was teaching Air Force pilots to fly jets in Tucson. Under some tutelage from Cottingham, Rande later became one of the best freefall photographers in the country.

Another friend was Bob Taylor (B.T.). Bob was the kind of jumper you could put on a dive anywhere you needed someone and when you got in, you could look around the formation and there was Bob, in and flying his assigned position without fuss or drama of any kind. B.T. wasn't flashy but he was solid.

Beech load at The Gulch, circa 1973. L to R Back: Bob Taylor, Pat Melroy, Matt Farmer, **, Jim Captain,**,Ron Luginbill, Dead Dugan. Front: Randy DeLuca, Bob Shaffer, Gary Hod Sanders, Dave Sheldon.   Photographer unknown.

Flashier but just as solid was Dave Sheldon, a jumper from Michigan who, much like us, had just packed up and moved to The Gulch. Sheldon was a small Midwest drop zone relative worker, and we got along well.

Two other friends at The Gulch were "Jeff Jacuzzi" (Geoff Frangos) and Bullit (sic) Bob. Geoff was an odd little guy who found The Gulch and decided to live on the drop zone full-time. Bullit Bob was even odder. Both had a macabre sense of humor. Bullit Bob was a talented artist and actually appreciated Jacuzzi's humor. For reasons known only to Bullit, he often jumped with a pair of Dracula teeth in his mouth. It was hard to imagine either one being tolerated on any other drop zone, but we were glad to be on a drop zone that tolerated both. We figured if these guys could jump here, Hell, we'd be golden.

Jacuzzi was given a desiccated human right arm and hand (God, if anyone, knew where it came from). As a joke, Jacuzzi buried the arm sticking out of the desert next to the entrance road to the airport and put a rusty rip cord in the desiccated hand next to a sign saying, "GO IN HERE." "Go in" was skydiver slang for being killed jumping. It was an unsettling welcome to The Gulch, but not as much as The Gulch Airways' slogan: "We fly; you die" which Bullit painted right on the side of the jump-planes.

Welcome to The Gulch.
Photographer unknown

In response to the jumper fatalities at The Gulch, Jacuzzi and Bullit came up with the idea of computing a "Frap Factor" for each of the regular jumpers on the drop zone. "Frap" was skydiver slang for hitting the ground going too fast to survive. One's Frap Factor was a number expressing, in Jacuzzi's and Bullit's opinions, how likely they thought you were to frap.

That is, their estimation of how safe a jumper you were. The higher one's Frap Factor the more likely they thought you were to get killed jumping. It was a creative and humorous way to bring up a very serious and not often discussed subject.

Once Jacuzzi and Bullit had everyone's Frap Factor, they came up with the "Bounce Index." "Bounce" is yet another skydiver slang term for being killed jumping. The Bounce Index was a ranking of Frap Factors such that the person with the highest frap factor would have a bounce index of 1 (most likely to bounce) and so on to the lowest Frap Factor and highest Bounce Index number; usually, depending on the number of jumpers hanging out at The Gulch, somewhere in the 20's. One wanted a low Frap Factor and a high Bounce Index. If you started creeping down the Bounce Index toward 1, it was time to rethink your skydiving equipment and conduct. The surest ways to move down the Bounce Index was to start jumping unproven or experimental equipment and pulling low.

Speaking of which, Jim Baker became the first (and only) person ever grounded for pulling low at The Gulch. This dubious honor sent his bounce index number plummeting toward 1 and prompted an unprecedented intervention by the rest of us. What no doubt saved him was that Larson grounded him for a whole month. The grounding gave Jim a chance to do some solo backpacking in the Superstition Mountains to get his head straight.

Formation Flying

One of the Homegrown's favorite dives early on at The Gulch was a nine-diamond. The formation was just toddler steps away from building stars, but nobody, at that time, had ever seen anything but a circle coming out of the sky so the diamonds got a lot of attention.

Ron Luginbill was often the point of the diamond. We could complete a nine diamond in as little as twenty seconds

9 Diamond. From left to right and front to back: Rich Fiegel, Matt Farmer, **, **, Ron Luginbill, Gary 'Hod' Sanders, Pat Melroy, Jim Baker, B.J. Worth.
Photo by Ray Cottingham ©1975

after exit, so Ron, at the point, had another twenty or thirty seconds of freefall being held by both feet doing nothing but waiting for break-up altitude when everyone would let go and separate to open their chutes (a group separation procedure known as "save yourself").

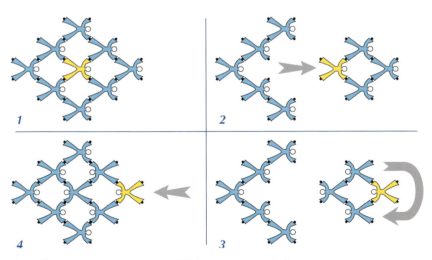

Diamond Dock: 4-way separates; turns 180 degrees; returns; docks

The idea that time spent falling in a finished formation was precious time lost was a major factor in the development of sequential relative work (doing a coordinated sequence of formations, instead of just one per jump). Ron had an idea for a beautiful nine-diamond sequence. Ron noticed that incorporated within the nine-diamond was a complete four-diamond that could be released from the nine-diamond, fly out as a unit, turn around and then fly back to rebuild the nine-diamond with the point of the four-diamond (Ron) now in the center of the rebuilt nine-diamond. The diamond-dock sequence became the progenitor of the film, *Wings* (available for viewing on YouTube).

In those days, we would draw skydiving formations using little stick figures. Ernie Bob and I worked as construction laborers at a huge subdivision going up outside Phoenix. We found the unfinished sheetrock walls of the new houses perfect for drawing stick-figure skydiving formations and trying to understand how they could best be sequenced. The painters must have wondered.

Doing relative work with formations, instead of as individuals, was a whole new idea. The Homegrown were enthusiastic about Ron's dive and put it up (attempted it) immediately. It went smoothly, with the separating four-diamond turning to do relative work as a unit providing all involved with stimulating visuals. The four jumpers doing relative work as a unit reported great satisfaction in flying hooked up with others rather than alone. The dive was considered a complete success.

More and more sequential relative work jumps followed, with the Homegrown forming the core and inviting others along to build a particular formation or sequence.

It was a time of great imagining and daring relative work never before attempted by anyone. Jim Captain came up with a 12-way sequence we called "quadra bi-poles to a cluster." To build the bi-poles required four jumpers to fly into the

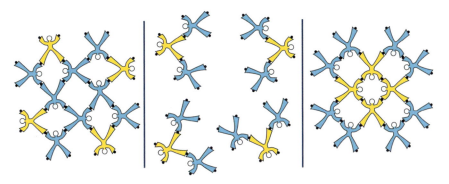

12-way jewel to (4) 3-way wedges to cluster.

formation backwards, that is, to make their final glide flying feet first while looking over their shoulder to judge their relative position to the formation. The four interlocked bi-poles were so intricate that we nicknamed the formation "The Jewel." The sequence to the cluster required simultaneously breaking the jewel into four 3-way wedges that then did relative work with each other to form the cluster. The sequence is filmed by Ray Cottingham in *Wings* (available on You Tube).

Thus, many jumps were firsts of some kind or another. Some, especially after USFET (United States Freefall Exhibition Team) was formed, resulted in national or world record skydives.

Wings and Beyond

Among the skydivers at The Gulch interested in the developing movement to formations and sequential relative work was B.J. Worth. B.J. was an accomplished skydiver who knew the who's who of skydiving, knew how to organize jumpers and could get things done. One of the who's B.J. knew was Carl Boenish. Carl was an avid California skydiver and producer of popular skydiving films (*Masters of the Sky*; *Sky Capers*; both available on You Tube). B.J. and Carl came up with the idea of making a film about the sequential and formation relative work being done at The Gulch.

The Homegrown were all for making a film and spent weekends from then on doing jumps specifically for that purpose. We lived the life of freefall derelicts, working at menial jobs in Phoenix all week and spending everything we made on jumps at The Gulch the next weekend. At the time, it was the most exciting and fulfilling life imaginable.

After 6 months or so of filming, B.J. Worth helped Carl put together the skydiving film *Wings* from the hours of raw footage shot during hundreds of skydives. *Wings* had skydives that were beyond anything most skydivers had even imagined possible, let alone seen or done. Showing this film to other skydivers and seeing their enthusiastic reactions led to performing exhibition jumps as the USFET at other drop zones and events. More skydivers were then able to see this new visually stunning skydiving.

At the 1974 Scrambles Meet in Elsinore, CA, Gulch skydivers built a 16-diamond using two Twin Beeches. We then flew a 9-diamond out of the 16-diamond, turned it around and flew it back to re-form the big 16-diamond. The 9-diamond was the largest formation ever to do relative work as a connected formation at that time. Then, it was on to the 1974 National Sport Parachuting Championships in Tahlequah, Oklahoma for more exhibition jumps.

USFET performed exhibition jumps demonstrating sequential relative work throughout the Nationals in Tahlequah, OK. Formations included a 16-man diamond, breaking into four 4-man diamonds that redocked into a cluster flake.

Mike Larson had flown a Twin Beech from The Gulch to Tahlequah but, of course, couldn't use it there during the competition. Always the entrepreneur, Mike found an agreeable airport in nearby Wagoner, OK and began flying loads for the crowd of skydivers hanging around but not competing in the nationals. The impromptu drop zone soon became a sequential

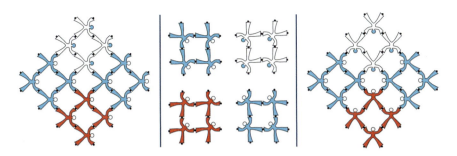

16-way diamond-split to 4-way diamonds; rotate to join leads into center circle; sides form cluster.

relative work hotspot. USFET members conducted what amounted to an advanced sequential relative work seminar for interested skydivers from all over the country.

After the meet ended, Gulch divers recruited other skydivers from among the attendees, including many of our old friends from Texas, and successfully completed a world record 25-diamond.

USFET exhibition jumps were in preparation for a B.J. Worth-organized trip to the 1975 Federation Aeronautique Internationale (FAI) World Skydiving Championships in West Germany. The team introduced sequential relative work to an appreciative audience and the trip was a huge success.

The world skydiving community was enthusiastic about sequential relative work that was to them a new and completely unimagined form of skydiving. The French were especially interested in the 4-man sequences they saw in *Wings*. They persuaded us to walk through the sequences with them on the ground (dirt dive). Within a few years, French teams were winning the World Meet in the 4-man event. One of the winning French teams was all-woman, and they immediately demanded the name of the event be changed from 4-man to 4-way, which is still in use today.

The FAI leadership was concerned that this new kind of relative work might develop into competition forms they did

1975 World Skydiving Championships, Warendorf, West Germany. Matt Farmer, Jim Baker, Ron Luginbill.   Courtesy of Jim Baker

not understand and therefore could not effectively regulate or incorporate into their existing championships. They reached out to the USFET for help. One member of USFET, Skratch Garrison (no relation to J.G.), was a certified FAI judge and well known to the FAI people at the World Meet.

Skratch was a good friend, spiritual mentor, and fellow "smooth and pretty" advocate. He knew I'd spent a good deal of time and energy developing 4-person sequential relative work sky dives with Jim Captain, Pat Melroy and Ron Luginbill. Skratch, as an FAI judge, was well aware of the difficulties the ten-man speed star competition model had placed on skydivers from other countries. Skratch had been advocating for a 4-person relative work competition for years. In fact, one of the reasons I had gone to the trouble of developing 4-person sequences in Casa Grande, was that I remembered an article Skratch had written years before advocating the advancement of 4-person relative work because of the wide availability of 4-place aircraft. Logical, but logic came late (well behind testosterone) to skydiver competition.

The FAI chairman, Eilif Ness, invited Skratch to come visit him in Norway after the World Meet to discuss the future form of skydiver competition. Skratch suggested to Eilif that I should be invited as well because of my technical expertise in sequence design. Some sequences just work better than others and it takes a while to find out which is which.

Immediately after the world meet, Skratch and I were stuffed into a European junker car, one of several transporting the Norwegian skydiving team. We went to catch the North Sea ferry at Homberg. We were pulling into the ferry port in Stockholm the next morning when a heated discussion broke out among the Norwegians. We Americans were asked to switch cars so that as many Norwegian cars as possible could have American passengers when they went through Swedish customs.

It turned out that each car was trying to smuggle booze into Norway where it is heavily taxed, very expensive and hard to find. The Norwegians believed the Swedish inspectors would be distracted by the American passports and the scruffy-looking people who owned them. This was near the end of the Vietnam war and Sweden was fed up with the flood of young penniless American draft-dodgers who had sought refuge in Sweden. The Norwegians figured the inspectors would hold up the customs line so long messing with the Americans that they would end up waving the other cars (with the booze) through to try to get the line moving again, and that's just what happened.

We stayed with the Ness family in a big house in a small town on the south coast of Norway for a couple of weeks, learned to drink aquavit, taught the Ness family American slang and idioms, and began the job of looking for a more widely accessible form of sequential relative work competition.

This effort narrowed to consideration of 4-person and 8-person sequences that demonstrated relative work flying skill and strong situational awareness while in freefall. Gone from consideration altogether was the time between first exit and last entry.

In this way, it was hoped 4-person sequences might help create a world competition model that would be accessible to skydivers on small drop zones with 4-place aircraft. Dedicated relative workers on small drop zones could enjoy working to be competitive in 4-person sequential and then combine their skills with another 4-person sequential team and be competitive as an eight-person sequential team. In this way, access to larger aircraft might become much less of a factor in skydiving competition. As it turned out, it was access to vertical wind tunnels that proved most important for skydiving competition going forward. Which goes to show, you never can tell.

We found The Gulch closed when we got back to Arizona. There was a Beech at the neighboring drop zone at Coolidge, Arizona, but it just wasn't the same, for some reason. A number of USFET members did, however, travel to the new and posh drop zone at Pope Valley, California for a DC-3 weekend and some of the old magic was back.

At an all-night acid-fueled discussion of the philosophy of skydiving with Jim Captain, Skratch, B.J. Worth and me, B.J. announced his desire to form an 8-way sequential competition team to compete under the new sequential rules being formulated by the FAI. Initial jumps were to be at Coolidge, AZ.

Ten years after deciding to ignore club rules in Saigon and try freefall relative work, I had thousands of relative work jumps. In an article for an Australian parachuting magazine, I had this to say about the highlights of my experience with freefall over those ten years:

"Freefall has always been a special place to me. A place where I can relate to others in new, different ways. An environment that's as constant as the pull of gravity and the cohesive integrity of air. A special place; one of balance and motion and people.

The freefall environment places no limits on you save the distant hard ground which is why you have a parachute. In freefall we are free as we can never quite be anywhere else. Free to do what we will. Free, since freefall itself places no limit on us, to see more clearly our own limits of skill and imagination. Freefall makes the sky a mirror. A mirror we can hold up to ourselves and see reflected a true image.

I remember ten years ago standing in the door of an old CH-34 helicopter with a young Aussie named Wally Morris. We were trying to hook-up with each other in freefall. It was a demanding task and I remember even now the quality of the feelings between us as we tried and missed. Tried and worked with each other and the air, until finally we were holding a hook-up. Smiling at each other as the warm Vietnamese air screamed the joy of accomplishment in our ears.

Wally and I were limited by our skill and imagination to a hook-up. It required all the relative work ability we had to do it, and we looked no further.

Just a few years later, I was in a five-man star over a small Kansas farm turned D.Z. We had tried to do a 5-man for six months; once each weekend. Stuffing five jumpers into a battered, 4-place Cessna 180 and struggling off our short dirt strip and up to 8500 feet, we tried hard to catch each other. One beautiful sunset August day we did… and made faces at each other around the circle and stuck out our tongues. We screamed all the way to the ground under parachutes and then laughed and slapped each other on the back while we spilled beer all over the place. The five-man star was a Kansas state record and much harder to do than my first hook-up with Wally but it was really the same thing: all those involved in both jumps put all they had into doing the dive, and that's what matters; not the size or geometry of the formation and certainly not how fast you can rush through it.

Later still, it was ten-man stars in Waco, Texas. We sang "Shall We Gather at The River" when we lined up at the door on jump run. It was a team that had consistency at a time when just doing five 10-mans in a row would win any meet outside California.

Back home in Kansas, I remember just coming out of a back-loop and knowing with a glance at the other four guys, sensing before it happened, that this time, we had it: Five-man, back loop, five-man from 7500 ft. We even had time to hold it; look once around the star at everyone's face before breaking off to open parachutes. On the way down there was a lot of shouting. We were getting better. We were getting faster. But that's not what we were shouting about. We could now do in the sky what we saw in our minds, and that is what made all the difference.

Then, when sport-wide star skills had built to a climax, some very imaginative people in Seattle started thinking up and doing non-round skydives. We saw a small piece of film at a parachute meet in California. It was incredible. Triple diamonds, a ten-man wedge and, a beautiful, big, 20-way "quadra-Pod". Man, those guys were good!

We stayed up all night getting stoned with and talking with the Seattle guys. By dawn we had a whole new way of thinking about relative work. The Homegrown were done racing each other to the circle. We already knew smooth and pretty flying; now we had something to apply it to.

Then it was on to Casa Grande, Arizona, where we planned and built, among other formations, some nice nine-man diamonds. Geometry and stickmen drawn on paper. We made the drawing of the nine-diamond real by opening a three-man star to a line, then filling in from both sides to make the diamond (try drawing it out with little stickmen; it's fun). There was time to hold the diamond forever. It felt different. It felt good! We didn't really know what we were doing, but we were doing it nonetheless.

After that, there were four-man dives at Casa Grande where we worked out the bases and mechanics of what we vaguely called "sequential relative work." There were "bi-poles" and "doughnuts" and "accordions" and "flying stair steps." There were funnels and spins, take outs, wrong grips, lost grips, mental errors, flying errors, tempers, disappointment and discouragement. But then, at first slowly, then more and more, there were stable formations and smooth transitions. Balance, timing, precision, smiles, joy and shouts of laughter across a sunlit Arizona sky. We were learning formation skydiving to be sure, but learning about ourselves and each other as much as anything else.

We had a chance to put our new hard-earned skills to good use that winter, when four of Seattle's most talented and imaginative fliers (the Clear Eye Express World Champion 4-man team) traveled two thousand miles to enter the annual "Chute-Out at The Gulch" skydiving meet with us. They came, they said, because they had seen a picture of one of our nine-man diamonds in *Spotter* magazine and didn't know anyone else did that sort of thing. The "Chute-Out" was a ten-man speed-star meet but, none of us being speed-star people, we decided to ignore the rules and just have fun doing sequential relative work during the meet instead of speed-stars. It felt like something symbolic was happening.

For the next four days we skydived. SKYDIVED!! Every jump a test. A test of our growing faith in each other. A test of our flying skill and imagination.

We completed a long, fast-moving, hard-flying sequence we only half-jokingly called "Dare to Be Great."

We built and flew the first ever five-point donut flake and tracked away five cats.

In one crazy complicated skydive we imagined we could build a six man in-out and a bi-pole hooked together; then roll the bi-pole around the in-out like two meshed gears. We tried it. It funneled. We lost the meet and won something I can't quite put a name on. But time was up, the meet was over... ahead...long drives home ... and jobs. Just time for one sunset dive: a double diamond dock.

We had tried the sequence two days ago during the meet. A hook-up with two four-man diamonds building separately 30 feet out on either side of it. That time one diamond had flown those 30 feet and docked on the hook-up; the other had missed and fallen low. The sequence made it clear to anyone watching that not everyone on a skydive need race each other to make a single round formation.

Now we tried it again, ten of us in an empty sky over a deserted D.Z. Even before those two diamonds had finished their swoop to simultaneous fingertip docks (not hitting the formation with any excess momentum), I knew it would happen. Happen because we all held the same picture of what would happen in our minds. Happen because each of us was present in the moment and directed all the relative work skill we had acquired toward that image.

Skydives are like that when your ability catches up with your imagination. These dives, some before, more since, have been peak dives. Dives where my friends and I have made real flying that until then had been done only in our minds.

Skill and imagination: an expanding, dynamic, human system. You imagine better flying skills and so you learn them. You learn better flying skills and so feed your imagination. One pulls, the other pushes and relative work expands and grows to try and fill the potential of people flying together in a limitless sky just for the freedom and joy of being there.

Sequential relative work was brand new. Jumpers wanted to know what it was and why it was turning their speed-star world upside down. I explained it this way for Pat Work's book: "Sequential Relative Work exists only because it is possible within the freefall environment. It is not the preconceived idea of any one group or individual. It is a natural step in the evolution of relative work. Sequential relative work is bounded only by the physical realities of freefall and our own skills and imagination. The sequence is the means. The joy of sequential is the flying necessary to accomplish it. Relative Work is a human possibility-a potential. Sequential is the pattern of the resulting flow."

Having taken skydiving from small drop zone parachuting in nowhere Kansas to international skydiving in West Germany and from small stars to cutting edge formation skydiving, we found ourselves back at The Gulch with no shared vision of what to do next. The Homegrown, without acrimony or bad vibes, splintered and went their separate ways.

After more than a decade, I'd had enough of chasing the skydiving dream full-time, so I put my chutes back in my parachute bag for the last time and moved to the Arizona mountains to learn how to ski and to continue to rock climb.

BOB (ERNIE BOB) JOHNSON

High school graduation was two months in the rear-view mirror and all the confusion that goes with it. It was summer of 1968 and a good number of my classmates had received draft notices. Their post-graduation vacation was going to be in SE Asia, getting a sun tan, drinking weird beer and chasing willing, gorgeous Asian babes who loved Americans. I didn't buy it. In spite of the fact that I had zero interest in more school, which I had grown to consider being legalized prison, I was considering the only known route to avoiding the aforementioned vacation: college.

My parents had some friends who had a son a couple of years older than me who was a member of a fraternity at Kansas State University, a mere 60 miles from my hometown of Salina, KS. Somehow, the topic of my future had come up, and they suggested that their son invite me to a fraternity "rush party." That's an event where blue bloods already enlisted, regale you with stories of the same beer, women and suntans as the military was offering, only with no rules, whatsoever. Sounded a little too good to be true, but I was assured that there was great food, lots of beer and an assortment of bikini clad girl friends of the members. The venue was a lake party with fast ski boats. I agreed.

I showed up after an hour's drive with a guy I didn't know and was relieved to get out of the car. As promised, there were beer, women and ski boats. I sat around swilling enough beer that I didn't mind the awkward nature of the whole thing. A guy came by and asked if I wanted to try my hand at some skiing. I had enough previous experience to be able to slalom, (one ski) and it was a hundred goddamn degrees, so I readily agreed. Once on the hot ski boat, the captain announced,

"Alright, who's next?"

I jumped up and so did this muscular, Italian looking dude and we donned life jackets and jumped in. We hadn't said hello, kiss my ass, or anything else, but made eye contact as the boat positioned and we adjusted our skis. He nodded. I gave the thumbs up and away we went. We no more than reached plane than he is giving the captain the thumbs up for more speed. Good by me. Then again and again until we are screaming at high speed and swooping each other, laughing our butts off as we went. Occasionally, one of us would spectacularly crash (it was always the Italian dude as I recall) and the occupants of the boat would cheer loudly. After 30 minutes or so, we were pretty well exhausted and headed to the beach for a beer. I had already bonded with this maniac to a certain degree. He stuck out his hand and said, "Kent Farney." Thus began a lifelong friendship and my path to skydiving.

Kent became my college fraternity brother and roommate. He already had 20 or so jumps and some cheap military parachuting equipment. He kept telling me how exciting it was and insisted that I go to the drop zone with him to watch. Eventually I did, with the promise that we'd hang out in Lawrence to do a little good-natured womanizing. So away we went, eventually going down a gravel road and arriving at an old farm house. I couldn't help but notice a serviceable looking C-180 parked nearby. I was more than casually familiar with aircraft as my dad was a career corporate pilot for a grain magnate headquartered in Salina. Some of my earliest memories were trying to look out the side window of a C-195, then trips with dad in the C-310.

The wind was blowing hard, so no jumping was going on. We sauntered up to the house, walked in and four or five hippie-looking guys were sitting around smoking pot. They greeted Kent and eyed me suspiciously. There was some small talk exclusively about jumping in skydiving lingo that I had a very hard time making any sense of. Eventually, near sundown, the wind subsided and the four of them strapped on some parachutes, loaded the plane and disappeared.

Some 15-20 minutes later the far away drone of the airplane became more pronounced and was finally visible above us. Suddenly, the engine cut, backfired a couple of times and four tiny black dots could be seen falling to earth. The wind had completely subsided and it was dead still. I'll never forget the sound of them falling that got louder and louder as they got lower and lower. They appeared to be milling around and finally two of them connected. I had noticed that one of them hadn't been milling at all, but was hanging out waiting for the first two to hook up. They were getting low now and the sound of them falling was akin to that of a jet engine. At the moment the two connected, the guy hanging out quickly and smoothly shot across the remaining distance and made it a three-person circle. It was a thing of beauty. They quickly separated, moved away from each other and the sound of parachutes opening replaced the jet noise. After that, the only sound was a gentle rustling of nylon as they made their way home. One of them came cruising right over the top of us, hooked the parachute close to the ground and landed lightly within about 50 feet of me. That was my first of many experiences of Matt Farmer, and my introduction to skydiving. I'll never forget that evening at Sky High drop zone outside of DeSoto, KS.

It was the Fall of 1969. Winter set in and Kent continued to make an occasional jump. I was enthralled by his stories as he progressed into freefall skydiving. Primarily because of that unforgettable evening, Kent was bugging me to give it a try. He actually gave me specific instructions on what a first jump would require. Finally, being too cheap to pony up the $35 to go to Sky High for a first jump, we concocted a not so believable story that I had made a first jump out at Ft Riley, a nearby army base. Away we went to Sky High with a bullshit story that no one at a regular drop zone would have fallen for, but Sky High was no normal drop zone. Matt Farmer sized me up along with the story and said, "How about we go inside and talk this over a little bit."

He gave me a lesson on a chalkboard about canopy control that I remember to this day. In fact, it probably saved my life more than once in the ensuing years. We went up later that day and I made my first static line jump, but more importantly, got introduced to a sport and a group of people who changed my life forever.

Learning to Fly

With Kent getting more and more hooked on the exhilaration of skydiving, it was impossible to escape the vortex myself. With Doc's (Kent's) addiction dictating how he spent weekends, I found myself also wanting to learn to fly (the skydiving lingo for doing relative work). I became Doc's sidekick for trips to Sky High and progressed rapidly through the process of learning the art of freefall. One of many "ah-ha" moments was experiencing the "buoyancy" of terminal velocity. Maneuvering came naturally shortly thereafter. Once Matt, Doc and the other more experienced skydivers became aware of my basic abilities to fall stable, be aware of the other jumpers around me and save myself when the RW was over, I was quickly accepted and invited on their loads. The learning curve was steep as a result of being in the air with Matt and Doc.

About that time, Doc and I became aware of some jumping going on closer to our home base at KSU in Manhattan, KS. A die-hard parachutist named Dave Snyder was operating a hit and miss DZ at Wamego, KS just a short drive away. We began jumping there at every opportunity, including impromptu sunset loads during the week. Two of the mainstay jumpers and solid RW guys were Roger Kidd and Leon Wolfe. We made several jumps with them in a relatively short time.

My skydiving skills were sharpening quickly and I was now considered one of the better flyers at Wamego. My first hookup was with Doc and Little Joe on my 21st jump back at Sky High. My old log book records that I closed a 3 man on my 25th jump. By then, I was hopelessly addicted to the fulfillment of my boyhood dreams of flying. My arms were my wings, my legs my rudder.

Matt had heard a rumor back in Kansas of a big relative work meet being held in Zephyrhills, FL at the same time as the 1970 Collegiate Nationals in Deland, FL. After attending the Collegiate meet, Matt drove over to Z-hills and Doc, Dave McFadden and I flew over to check it out. I think I remember the relative work meet was over and we didn't hang around for long. We did, however, learn there had been a half dozen 10-man speed star teams at the meet, including some hot California teams. Little did we know that one year later the Kansas Homegrown would be born in the form of a 10-man pick up team with the legendary Jerry Bird and a handful of his California speedsters.

The Awakening

That trip to the 1970 Collegiate Nationals proved to be the first step in a path that would culminate at The Gulch some four years later. After arriving back in KS, all we could talk about was what we had run across in Z-Hills that Thanksgiving. Although we arrived after the event, it was clear the best relative workers in the world had come together to compete and share the rapidly advancing art form of RW. Even though we were an obscure bunch of outlaws in the middle of nowhere, we came back knowing that our obsession with freefall relative work was shared nationally. Our commitment to RW went to the next level. We were jumping with even greater shared purpose.

Doc and I continued gaining experience by chasing some of the other skydivers at Wamego and Herrington around the sky. It was good training. Skills sharpened and when we got together with Matt at Sky High, the quality of our jumps was noticeably improving. Matt mentored a young, amiable pilot who quickly turned into a first-rate skydiver.

The story of the Homegrown cannot be told without telling the story of Herb Conley. Herb lived at the Desoto drop zone with Matt and the other commune members. Matt and Herb were kindred spirits and defined what friendship is really about. The four of us, Doc, Herb, Matt and myself had a connection in the air and on the ground. Our skydives together became smooth. Our zero momentum four-man stars were quick and clean every time. After a day of jumping, we would retreat to the farmhouse to smoke homegrown and engage in deep discussions about the art form of the flying we were experiencing together.

One night, Matt handed me a small paperback and said, "Check this out; it's what we are chasing." The name of that book was *Jonathan Livingston Seagull* by Richard Bach. It is the story of an outlaw seagull whose obsession with pushing the limits of flight made him an outcast from the flock. He eventually enlisted disciples and together they pushed the boundaries not just of flight, but of imagination.

The book became the Homegrown's scripture. The essence of the book that we related to our RW efforts was captured in the one powerful statement: "Perfect speed, Jonathan, is being there". It defined our quest perfectly. No longer were we thinking of our flying in terms of only speed.

Herb Heads to Elsinore, CA

None of us can recall the details of Herb heading west to check out what was happening in Elsinore, CA the fall of 1971. What we do know is that Herb's magnetic personality and some of our good Homegrown weed made him a welcomed newcomer at the drop zone. He jumped with some of the best skydivers there, including Jerry Bird. They apparently became friends quickly. Herb undoubtedly shared our relative work efforts back in KS with Jerry and upon return from his trip, Herb shocked us all with the announcement that Bird had suggested that he bring some of his California speedsters to join the four of us (Matt, Herb, Doc and myself) to compete in the Z-Hills Turkey meet. The team would be named the "Kansas Homegrown."

That assumed, of course, that we could jerk our shit together and show up in Florida-no small thing since we were all generally near broke most of the time. We figured out how to get there (I believe we'd 've walked if necessary) and showed up wide eyed and ready to rock.

Matt, Herb and Jim Captain, a talented young student who had an obvious passion for RW, natural flying ability and never flinched at any of our overtly outlaw attitudes, made their way via car. Doc and I flew down in Doc's Dad's C-182.

Since we had never jumped out of anything but small Cessnas, and knowing that the competition would be out of Twin Beeches and DC-3's, Doc and I detoured south to look for a rumored outlaw drop zone outside of Waco, Texas where they were said to have a Twin Beech. Sure enough, after some cruising around the Waco area, we spotted an all-white Twin Beech sitting next to a small grass strip outside Valley Mills, Texas.

We landed, hoping to explain our plight and get some practice exits out of their Beech. What we found was a small group of obvious counterculture dudes shooting various guns into a large pit in the ground (It's a Texas thing?). As fate would have it, they were members of a 10-man speed star team called "The Valley Mills Turtles" who were themselves planning to head to Z-Hills for the same meet we were headed to. An obvious karmic entanglement.

Bob Johnson and Kent Farney, 1972.   Photo courtesy of Bob Johnson

After introductions and explaining what we were up to, the DZ operator, Gary Lewis, was more than happy to fire up the Beech and get us the needed experience we were after. We geared up and loaded into the shopworn-looking Twin Beech. I noticed Gary, who was the owner and pilot, was carrying a plastic Coca Cola bottle full of some sort of liquid (obviously not Coca Cola) with him as he made his way to the cockpit. I was focused on my upcoming jump so didn't think much of it. I found out later that the mystery liquid was brake fluid that he poured in the brake cylinders just before landing because otherwise the leaking brake cylinders would be empty and there would be no brakes.

Since there were only five of us on the load, the climb to 7,500 ft was quick. They let Doc and me go last, since that was the whole purpose.

Engines cut, "Ready, set, go!!" I was plastered to Doc during the short fast shuffle to the door and tripped just as I was about to launch out the door, falling flat on my face! Everyone was gone and all I could do was crawl to the door and roll out. Needless to say, I was immediately ass over elbows and only gained control after several seconds. I had just gone last on the longest Beech exit in history. I was completely disoriented and could see no other skydivers, airplane, NOTHING.

I couldn't see anything on the ground that resembled the drop zone either. I tracked, keeping my eyes peeled for opening parachutes, but saw none. I pulled at what I thought was about two grand. Floating down I still saw nothing that would help me figure out where the hell I was. I landed near a road and was walking up the road with my chute folded between my arms when a local rancher stopped and asked me if I needed a lift to the airport. He was used to seeing derelict skydivers and knew right where to take me.

When I arrived, the Texas guys wanted to know where the hell I'd gone. Since I had tracked so far, they hadn't even seen my chute open and feared that I had burned in. I quickly fabricated a story that Doc had kicked me squarely in the jaw on exit (we wore no helmets back then) and knocked me semi-unconscious. It was, I told the Texans, only due to my iron will and ability to focus under extreme duress that I was able to survive.

They seemed to be happy I was alive, thereby avoiding the scrutiny of authorities that would have resulted from my death. Doc and I made five jumps over the next two days with the Texas boys that began lifelong friendships that exist to this day.

Then on to Z-Hills.

As we taxied up to the tarmac in the C-182, Matt came strolling up to greet us. "You guys aren't going to believe what's going on here. It's RW ground zero!"

His words were prophetic. We unloaded and dragged sleeping bags over to join Matt, Herb and Captain. The excitement was palpable. None of us could sleep much in anticipation of the jumping we knew was going to unfold. Although many memories of an experience that happened over 50 yrs. ago are hazy, there are a few details etched indelibly in my memory.

The first was watching what turned out to be the James Gang doing a practice jump. They made a very smooth 10-man, perfectly round, probably in about 25 sec. Their white jumpsuits with a dark blue Florida sky as backdrop made for dramatic visuals. To my surprise, they broke the 10-man they had just made, back looped in perfect synchrony and reformed a perfect 10-man snowflake!

I was blown away, as I'm sure everyone else watching was

1971 Z-HillsTurkey Meet Friendship Dive.L to R Standing: Hank Asciutto, Pat Works, Dana Parker, Jim Hooper, Al Krueger, Ron Cox, Rick Miller, John Sherman, Phil Smith, Skratch Garrison, Dick Parker, Bob Federman. Kneeling: Matt Farmer, Jim Mahr (Streak), Lou Jecker, Jack Peck, Dick Giarrusso, Ken Gillespie, Jim Baron.
Sitting: Herb Conley, Dave Arrington, Jerry Bird, T-Bow Smith (Bill).
Photo posted in Oldschool Skydiving Facebook by Nancy LaReviere.

too. It was the first sequential relative work I had ever seen from the ground and a no shit "ah-ha" moment.

Later that morning we met a ton of people including Jerry Bird and his friends from Elsinore that were to make up the Kansas Homegrown team. Pickup loads were being put together and we found ourselves on a couple of 16-man attempts with several of the James Gang team members as well: Pat Works, Jim Bohr, Bill Newell and others of equal stature.

I qualified for both my SCR and SCS (Star Crest Recipient and Star Crest Solo) on one jump with these guys. Somewhat surreal to think back on it. In checking my log books, I recorded 9 jumps in the next 3 days, 5 of them competition jumps on the newly formed and inaugural Kansas Homegrown team. The lineup, I think in rough order was Al Kruger base, Rocky Walker pin, Herb Conley, Doc Farney, myself, Security Bill Smith, Bill Covin, Matt Farmer, Jerry Bird and Pete Gruber.

I don't think we had a single practice jump. Our first competition jump was eye opening to say the least. We did a 19-second what I thought was a 10-man which, I was told by Bird after the jump, would have been a world record at the time. However, the base built so quickly that our pin-man missed Al, went low and never recovered, so we had only a 9-man.

That effectively eliminated us from any realistic chance of winning since at least two of the other teams, James Gang and Valley Mills Turtles made 10-mans routinely every time out. Nonetheless, we made some respectable 25-30 second ten-mans until the last jump where we managed only a chaotic 6-man. Because of clouds the meet was suspended. We thought skydiving was over for the day so had partaken in some serious toking of the homegrown which I'm certain had the predictable effect.

The meet concluded and the Valley Mills Turtles ended

up on top after the James Gang made a very uncharacteristic mistake on their last jump and failed to get a 10-man. The two top teams then went up to attempt a 20-man, which I think would have been a world record at the time. They fell just short before running out of altitude and tracking away. Everyone opened except one guy who was obviously intentionally humming it (sky diver lingo for an intentional low pull). It was the first time I had ever witnessed a low pull from the ground. Finally, after we were all convinced, he was going in, the guy waved off and pulled. His black and gold PC cracked as it opened at about 400 ft.!!

The daredevil made a perfect hook turn to a featherlight standup landing as the crowd loudly cheered. It was none other than Phil Mayfield, a member of the Valley Mills team and one of the Texas guys that Doc and I had met when we stopped there on our way to the meet. The drop zone operator, Jeff Searles, immediately confronted Phil and loudly announced, "You're grounded!!" The crowd cheered wildly again.

It was said that Phil had the honor of being the first person ever grounded for low pulling at Z-Hills. Phil survived many other low pull escapades and later became one of the very first BASE jumpers. He remains a close friend all these years later as have several of the original Valley Mills skydivers. Everyone who witnessed that jump remembers it to this day.

The meet ended shortly thereafter. We flew home and the next chapter in the evolution of the Kansas Homegrown began.

Back to Kansas

The experience in Z-Hills turbo-charged our energy. The steady path of improving skills and expanding imagination went to a new level. One of the takeaways from our Florida adventure was the realization that skydiving really is much better if you are doing it with other skilled jumpers. Another takeaway was that we had flown with arguably the best skydivers in the world and held our own very respectably. That realization added to the swagger we took back to Kansas.

Our first inclination was to go about connecting with other qualified jumpers in our region. Keep in mind that there were no cell phones and the means of communication remained largely word of mouth. On top of that, it was dead of winter in Kansas which meant sporadic weather and cold temps, sometimes really cold. We made jumps as we could, but the momentum from Z-Hills was waning.

I haven't been able to reconstruct the next few weeks, but it was the following February that tragedy struck at the very heart and soul of the Homegrown. Herb Conley was killed in a skydiving accident in Texas while visiting our new found friends in Valley Mills. Details to this day are sketchy, but the bottom line is that we lost a critical piece of the Homegrown family.

Matt was especially impacted. He and Herb were not only best friends, they were soulmate brothers and their synergy was the heart and soul of the Homegrown. All I really recall is sitting in Matt's apartment in Lawrence after the funeral. We didn't talk much; I suppose mostly because we didn't know what to say. After some joints went around, the conversation began to flow.

Matt took the lead and we talked about skydiving and relative work and Jonathan Livingston Seagull and Fletcher Gull and that "perfect speed" really is "being there."

The Homegrown grew up a little. The passion for flying that bonded us was never more palpable. And we carried on, without looking back, except to say, "Thank you, Herb. There would probably have never been a Kansas Homegrown without you."

Efforts to identify and connect with other competent skydivers started to get traction the next spring. There was a drop zone in Edgerton, KS that had a core of four or five experienced relative workers that we had heard of, but had not jumped with. Matt made a connection with them and we went about getting to know them the only way skydivers know how to do — we made some jumps with them.

Initially, we made some Cessna formation loads, but with talk of putting together a KS team for the upcoming 1972 Z-Hills boogey, we knew we needed to locate a small door Twin Beech. Enter Walt and his spit-shined bird that I believe Jim Baker came across.

Arrangements were made to meet Walt at Paola airport outside of Kansas City. He struck me as a quiet, serious aviator and competent enough to fly jumpers in an airplane that required a serious pilot. My log book indicates that we made six jumps with the first intended 10-man competition line up that first weekend. While we failed to make consistent 10-man stars, the jumps were reasonably smooth, orderly and showed enough promise that we were excited to line up additional weekends.

It was six weeks later before we could coordinate the next get together. Because of weather we were only able to make three jumps that weekend, but made our first newly formed team 10-man star in a respectable 30 seconds. Promising indeed, since most of us had very little experience exiting a small door Beech and even less at speed star competition. Again, it was several weeks before we could put the rag-tag team back in the air.

This time, Walt had a geeky looking, horn-rimmed glasses dude flying right seat. It was clear that Ted was no Walt. As it turned out Walt was giving him his first checkout ride in the Twin Beech. Our first takeoff roll with Ted trying to wrestle the Twin Beech off the ground was horrifying. I remember sitting just inside the bulkhead with Matt next to me. As the plane accelerated and the tail wheel came up, the tail began to wash side to side inhibiting the speed needed to rotate normally. Matt and I exchanged concerned glances. Most people who have spent much time in aircraft have a feel for when an airplane is ready to fly. As the takeoff roll dragged on, using what must have been nearly all of the runway, Ted struggled to get airborne. The stall warning began blaring and the airplane miraculously bounced into the air and flew about a full mile before getting enough speed to climb, the stall warning wailing the whole time. We proceeded uneventfully to altitude.

After getting on the ground after our jump, we were gathering in the packing area for our normal debrief. I singled out Matt and brought up the troubling takeoff roll. As team captain, Matt was totally in skydiving debrief mode and basically blew me off with his infamous quote, "Don't worry about it. If he loses it, he'll never get it off the ground far enough to kill anyone." These words proved to be prophetic.

I wasn't there for the next arranged weekend at Paola. Walt had become satisfied that Ted could manage flying solo for some reason that escapes me to this day. Ted did in fact lose control, stall on takeoff roll and spin off the end of the runway resulting in a spectacular sliding crash that Matt has previously described in detail.

I will now tell the story from my perspective having been watching the report of it on the evening news at my home in Salina.

Beech Crash from A Different Perspective

It seems to me that it was the next weekend since Ted had somehow become the head pilot of Walt's Twin Beech. I had gotten word that Roger Kidd and Leon Wolfe, previous skydiving pals who had tried out for and made the Army Golden Knights demonstration team two years earlier, were going to be in Salina, KS for an air show featuring the Thunderbirds.

Roger and I talked by phone and he invited me to come

out the day before the show to meet the team and some of the Thunderbird jet jockeys. I was anxious to catch up with them and thought maybe they could even snivel me a spot on some of their practice jumps. While that didn't happen, I had a good time meeting people and invited them over to my parents' house for some of my Dad's special occasion grilled steak.

They agreed and we had a leisurely evening of eating, beer drinking and catching up. My Dad, whose only passion greater than flying was my Mom, had been a flight instructor during the war and had subsequently become a full time corporate pilot for a large Midwest agricultural firm. He was especially enjoying the stories Roger and Leon were sharing.

They finally called it a night, and my Dad and I retired to the basement to watch TV and hang out. The local evening news was wrapping up when a special breaking news item interrupted the newscaster. A picture of an airplane fully engulfed in flames came on the screen and the caption underneath read something like this — "Plane carrying Skydivers Crashes."

The announcer immediately launched into the breaking news. "Details are just being released. A private plane carrying at least 8 people, including members of a local skydiving team has crashed and burned at the Paola, KS municipal airport. There is no report of survivors."

That moment will be forever etched in my mind. Sensory overload caused me to go completely numb. I was probably in shock. I couldn't wrap my mind around what I had just seen and heard. There were no details offered in the brief news report.

As the reality began to set in, a profound sense of sorrow settled over me. It had only been a few short months ago that the Homegrown had been rocked to our core by Herb's death. Back then I had had all my brothers around to share the grief with. Although I couldn't be sure who all was on that airplane, I knew it was most, if not all, of my Kansas Homegrown brothers. I had never felt so alone. Everything was totally dark.

My Dad tried calling the local FAA, but they had no further information. I tried calling Dave Snyder, the regional ASO (area safety officer), but no answer. I'm guessing about an hour had passed, and the phone rang. The voice on the other end was none other than Doc Farney!! My head exploded. I was certain he would have been on the load — and he was, along with Matt, Jim Baker, Jim Captain and a few of the Edgerton guys.

Doc filled me in on every detail of the crash. True to form, Ted had perfectly executed the incompetent takeoff run he had demonstrated on the previous loads I had been on the week before only this time he ran out of runway. He tried frantically to jerk the ship off the ground, but she stalled and pancaked back to earth, spinning out into the wheat field off the end of the runway, radial engines going full throttle. She came to rest with everyone in a tangled pile crammed into the tail of the plane.

A small flame trickled out of the cowling of one of the engines. Someone yelled "Fire!!" and everyone was able to scramble out and run to beat hell. The fire grew and suddenly the fuel tank in that wing exploded and the plane was consumed in flames immediately.

More importantly, he reported that no one got as much as a scratch. To my way of thinking, if there was such a thing as a miracle, this had to be it. In one short hour I had run the entire gauntlet of life's most extreme emotions from complete despair to unfathomable elation of getting my Homegrown brothers back from the dead. I had a hard time going to sleep that night, but remember lying in bed trying to digest the whole bizarre affair. After a while, a smile came across my face as I remembered Matt's prophetic words — "he won't get it high enough to kill anyone". I drifted off to sleep with a feeling of profound gratitude — and the thought that maybe we just really were bulletproof.

Next Stop Z-Hills '72

With no more local Twin Beeches in the offing (word of the "skydiver-caused crash" in Paola, which is how that lame chickenshit Ted portrayed it, didn't help) we resorted to our roots — formation Cessnas. We continued to assemble the 10-man team and make a limited number of practice jumps. As the lineup got solidified, the skydives, while inconsistent, showed flashes of actually being competitive. The enthusiasm for attending the annual Turkey Meet at Z-Hills grew, especially with the assumed "credibility" that a repeat visit from the Kansas Homegrown of the year before would seem to facilitate, at least in our own minds.

We had a team meeting at a well-known, upscale KC steakhouse to finalize details of the trip. It was memorable for reasons that were unexpected — the Edgerton contingency as characterized in How Crazy is Too Crazy (Part 2)

Matt had arranged for a series of demo jumps that originated at the Lawrence airport. They included tight rodeo arenas in high winds with "rags" (modified 5-TU military surplus parachutes) as well as an annual hippie fest that drew thousands each year called the "Big Eat". They went off flawlessly and as a result, the Homegrown was developing a reputation amongst the aviation community as a team of "expert" skydivers.

Matt sensed an opportunity to approach the Lawrence airport manager about allowing some weekend jumping with the understanding that it would not be open to the general skydiving community, but rather "invitation only" to expert skydivers who were competing nationally — a bit of a stretch, but mild compared to some of the stories we made up to find reliable airplanes to jump out of. Matt had to take personal responsibility for any mishaps, including any overtly derelict behavior that might embarrass the airport manager. No small thing in his mind, so it was made clear to invitees that it was a one strike and you are out policy. It was during this short time frame that some of our earliest ventures into what would later become the basis for "sequential" relative work occurred.

Synergy

The emergence of sequential skydiving was indeed a synergy between skill and imagination; a classic "strange loop" — each essential in the creation of the other. There was an unknown number of small, obscure drop zones scattered randomly around the world in the late '60s and early 70s and I think it's fair to say that, if the facts were fully known, many of them contributed to what culminated in the innovative skydives that the Kansas Homegrown spearheaded at The Gulch in '73, 74 and 75. The world was introduced to this new way of artistic expression by the United States Freefall Exhibition Team (USFET) organized at The Gulch by B.J. Worth with the assistance of Matt Farmer and others. Their exhibition jumps were captured in the video *Wings*, produced by Carl Boenish and filmed by Ray Cottingham in 1975. The sequential breakthrough had a lasting effect that continues to this day in the sport of relative work skydiving.

The Homegrown arrived at The Gulch in the late summer of '73. It was a drop zone that was every outlaw skydiver's dream come true: no rules to speak of, no safety officers, no required licenses, no reserve packing card checks, but with great jump aircraft, skilled pilots, a solid core of talented local skydivers, and plenty of overt looseness. The perfect climate for what transpired over the next three years.

There were many memorable and pivotal events that seemed to just occur organically at The Gulch in those early days. One of the first was what was referred to as the "Dale Evans Assigned Slot 20-man." Dale Evans was one of the freelance skydivers that showed up regularly and randomly at The Gulch. I believe he was from Louisiana.

We had only been at The Gulch a short time and were just getting recognized by the local A stringers as good skydivers. Dale came up with the idea of a 20-man skydive where there were specific assigned slots — no random "get in" when and where you can. This was a novel approach to building a star at that time. It was also the first time I recall doing a "dirt dive"— that is simulating an exit on the ground, flying to your quadrant, and waiting for your slot to be created by the jumpers in front of you.

We intuitively liked the idea and the first dirt dive was greeted by lots of smiles and camaraderie as we walked through the dive from start to completion. It was fun. Lots of fun. Now for the test. We loaded the Loadstar in the prescribed order and off we went.

I recall having a totally different mindset on the climb to altitude. The dive was designed to be a 5-man star that created 5 slots for the next ring of five skydivers who had positioned and waited for their assigned slot. Once everyone docked in their assigned place, there were now 10 new slots with the remaining 10 skydivers positioned to take those and complete the 20-man star. The skydive went perfectly as choreographed on the ground. The star built smoothly, stayed perfectly stable and was always never anything but nearly perfectly round.

I have a graphic memory etched in my brain as I flew to my position on the back side of the formation of the symmetry and order of the fluid positioning and building that was occurring in my field of vision. It was poetry in motion and everyone on the load experienced it. The energy on the ground afterwards was electric. We only got 19 on that jump as one of the late flyers went low and couldn't recover. No matter. We put that jump up again on four different occasions with mostly the same group and got 20 each time, the last being at the 1973 Turkey Meet at

The Gulch.

There was a broken low overcast at 2,000 ft that day that had kept the meet from starting. I believe it was Matt who convinced the drop zone owner/operator, Mike Larson, to let us put that load up despite the conditions. Away we went.

As before, the star built beautifully and by 4500 ft we were all in and humming it. No one was about to be the one to break before we went through the cloud layer and into full view of the crowd on the ground below. We all knew where that cloud layer bottom was, so immediately after popping through it, everyone broke and parachutes were flying like popcorn on a hot griddle. Most everyone was open between 500 and 1,000 ft. It was on this jump that Homegrown Jim Baker, who had been warned by Mike Larson for previous low pulls, made history by being the first and only person ever to be grounded at The Gulch.

As mentioned, there were many baby steps that led to the breakthrough at The Gulch in 1973 and over the next two years. I have always felt that what was experienced and clearly demonstrated by the Dale Evans assigned slot 20-man jumps were meaningful long strides. Quantum leaps were right around the corner.

We all struggled to find decent employment to support ourselves and our skydiving habit. Pat Melroy was an experienced carpenter and landed a construction gig with a large Phoenix development company. Not long after he started, he got Matt and me on the labor crew. We were literally digging ditches in 100+ degree weather to begin with. It was not long before we moved up the chain. Eventually, we worked together going through the nearly completed units and installing light fixtures, bathroom mirrors, door knob sets and many other miscellaneous finish details.

We spent a good deal of that time drawing stick men on the unpainted drywall of various skydives and formations that we had not yet attempted. A significant result of the scribblings were some basic formations: stars, diamonds, bi-poles, stair steps, caterpillars and wedges; then drawing larger formations with variations of these pieces. They looked very artistic and beautiful on the walls. Hieroglyphics, if you will.

We began making jumps from the C-180 doing sequences of these forms, initially by relying on grip switches. I remember the first time we decided to "fly" a diamond. The thought was to see if we could make controlled turns right and left and then "track" the diamond on heading. The answer came on the first attempt: Of course we could! That opened the door to a 9-man diamond that dropped grips and let a 4-man diamond back out, rotate 360 degrees and re-dock back to a 9-diamond. It took a few attempts, but soon became a signature jump that drew a lot of attention on the drop zone. Imaginations soared. Soon many other dives were designed and the birth of what is now referred to as sequential RW steadily emerged.

There was a strong collaboration with the group from Seattle who visited The Gulch regularly and who had introduced the Homegrown to some beautiful, non-round formations that they had photographed and filmed back at their home drop zone. They had independently been working on much the same techniques. The handwriting was on the wall (no pun intended!). A new, fun, and exciting form of skydiving grew rapidly around the country and the world. It was aptly called "sequential relative work."

JIM BAKER

My Senior Day in high school changed my life. That day my entire class spent the afternoon outdoors on our practice fields, partying and saying our goodbyes as we all headed off in new directions. Our class President announced that a group of skydivers would soon be flying overhead. He said they would jump out and "FLY" together before opening their parachutes; then land on an "X" made out of gym towels laid out on the ground. FLY! WTF. What do you mean Fly? Men don't FLY. I expected a group of guys in military fatigues, combat boots, and crew cuts. What I saw next changed my life.

That day we had a high overcast. Sure enough, a few minutes later I saw a single engine plane flying overhead and then three small black dots exit the plane. The overcast made it perfectly clear that these guys exited separately. Once they were in free fall, I watched them FLY together and hold hands in a star formation. I couldn't believe my eyes. THEY CAN FLY! Then, instead of army parachutes, they opened up with bright multi-colored maneuverable chutes. One of them was even shaped in a delta wing. They swooped around above our heads and finally did soft standup landings within a few feet of the center of the "X". I was standing just a few feet away. Instead of Army guys, three longhaired hippies whipped off their helmets to the roar of the crowd. While I hadn't yet made a jump, in that moment I became a skydiver.

I ran up to one of them and asked where can I learn to skydive. He mumbled Sky High Drop Zone. He probably did not want a bunch of knuckle-headed high school kids showing up at his drop zone. I think the drop zone was in its waning days of operation. He gave me the basic location of the DZ but in the days, weeks, and months following I was never able to find it.

I did not go directly to college. I spent the next year working and moving out of the house and running with the wrong crowd. I rented an apartment in Westport, doing too many drugs and nearly getting busted. It was a low time in my life. Not wanting drugs or jail time on my resume, I was ready to turn things around. I enrolled in KU for the fall semester in 71'. I fell in love with KU and college life. For the first time in my life, I loved school and was getting pretty good grades.

One day returning to my apartment, I drove by a guy packing a parachute outside of his apartment. It was Mike Canella. I pulled over, jumped out and ran up to him.

"Wow, man where can I learn to skydive? I've wanted to do this for more than a year."

He said the only place around was an airport in Herrington, KS. Later, I asked if my buddy Chuck Witthaus would like to join me and go together. He agreed and we made plans the next week to go the drop zone.

Sure enough, the next Saturday morning we were at Sky Sports in Herrington, KS. This was an old abandoned Army Air Force base just outside of town. We met Dave Snyder, the owner and pilot, paid him our $45 and spent the morning being trained by John Schuman. It just so happened that John planned to make his 500th jump that weekend and was in a festive mood.

After our ground training was completed, we got on the manifest and prepared to make our first jump. Unfortunately, Mother Nature stepped in and provided us with howling winds. We hung around all day hoping for them to calm down, but with no luck. At the end of the day, we drove back to Manhattan, KS and partied hard in Aggieville.

The next morning, shaking off our hangovers, we headed back to Herrington. Sadly again, the winds were blowing hard, so we sat around all day hoping to get our chance. As the day wound down, we were getting anxious, still hoping to get to jump. Finally, late that afternoon the winds began to calm down. Snyder came in and said we finally were on a load. Then three hot shot guys from the K-State Sky Diving Club showed up and the next thing we knew, we were bumped off the last load of the day. Holy Shit, Batman! I f-cking waited all weekend and these guys show up and bump us off. I'm a lover, not a fighter, but at that moment I was ready to kick ass and take names. These "hot shots," Ernie Bob Johnson, Kent Farney, and Scott Godding were not going to keep me from making my first jump.

On any other day, these guys would have whipped my ass, but not that day. I had been dreaming about this day for more than a year, and these guys were not going to deny me. I remember going nose to nose and making it perfectly clear that they were not going to bump us off the load. Snyder stepped in and they backed off. Scott Godding, who minutes before I was ready to do battle with, was going to be my jumpmaster. Wanting to kick your jumpmaster's ass just minutes before you go does not make for an easy plane ride up on your first jump. Well after sunset, on October 31, 1971, my 19th birthday, I made my first jump.

Over the following months, I spent every single weekend at the drop zone. I met Jim Captain and B.A. They helped me get in with Matt, Bob, and Kent (the good jumpers) and we began jumping with them. B.A. and I got very good at Base/Pin (first and second out the door) which helped us win our slots with the group. From that day, we have become best friends, a bond that has endured for nearly fifty years.

Fast-forward one year. I was in Matt Farmer's apartment in Lawrence, KS talking about skydiving when I discovered that Matt, who had become my very close friend, was the guy who had jumped the delta wing into my high school Senior Day. Until that time neither of us realized that we had shared that moment.

I was very lucky to be a part of the Homegrown. While I was not part of the original team, during my tenure we shared many great experiences. A partial list includes early KU airport eight-ways, several Texas Trips, the Beech Burn, Elsinore, Zephyrhills, Seattle, and of course "The Gulch", *Wings*, USFET, Mirror Image, and three World Teams.

Being a Homegrown was fundamental in helping me learn about being on and, later, leading teams. I have learned so much from Bob, Matt and Doc.

JIM CAPTAIN

I made my first parachute jump just a few weeks after my high school graduation in 1971. I spent the last semester of high school working the night shift stocking shelves at the local Safeway grocery store. The other guy on the night shift was Bobby Bettinger. One night, sitting in the cafeteria on our break, he told me I should come out to where he was living on a farm in Desoto Kansas. He said, "You need to check out what these guys are doing." He was referring to the parachute operation run by Matt Farmer: Sky High Skydivers.

At 18, I was up for just about anything. At the farm, I found a low-key couple of guys, Matt Farmer owner/instructor and Herb Conley, pilot/skydiver. They said parachuting lessons and my first jump would be $35, but not today, the plane was broken. I don't think they took me seriously; I looked pretty young and very straight compared to them with long hair. To me, the farm looked more like a commune.

I went back the next weekend, but they were busy working in the fields. They said come back next week. It was only a 25-to-30-minute drive, so I went back the next weekend and got my first jump instruction. It was June 12th, 1971. I don't remember much of it. Matt wrote some stuff on a blackboard and showed me the equipment. A couple hours later we were taking off for my first time in an airplane, a Cessna 180. It was all a new experience.

Sensory overload left me with very little recall of that first jump. I remembered how quiet it was floating down under the parachute. I went back the next day and made two more jumps. My second jump was much the same as the first except on landing, I hit feet, then butt, and my head slammed into a fence post. That was the first time I realized people can get hurt doing this.

That could easily have been my last jump, but I went up and did my third, a dummy rip cord pull (DRCP). I finished the standard jump progression of 5 static lines with 3 DRCP's and my first Clear & Pull (I think Matt said it was more of a Pull & Clear) on the 4th of July.

By now they were taking me more seriously and took me with them on a trip to Seagoville (Valley Mills) Texas. I logged it as a FF (Free Fall) and noted: "Tree Landing." It's possible my chute glanced against a large sage brush, not really sure.

When we went back to Kansas (now it's we), there was a new plane to jump. It was an old looking plane, a Stinson V-77 model. At this point I decided to keep jumping until I could make a 30 second delay. At least that's what I told my friends and parents who didn't understand why I was parachuting.

On one of the first few jumps out of the Stinson, something happened and the engine stopped. Thinking it was an emergency, I started scrambling for the door. Matt grabbed ahold of my shoulder and said RELAX.... We continued gliding towards the exit point and I was told to go. All I could think of as I fell away from the plane was what was going to happen to Herb? Airplanes were still pretty new to me and I had no idea they could glide and land without the engine running.

Getting past my first 30-second delay and finding I could fall stable most of the time, falling began to feel more like flying. It was at this point that parachuting became skydiving to me and was something I wanted to keep doing.

There were a couple of other important lessons I learned during the last days at Sky High in Desoto before a new highway was to be built through the center of the DZ. I learned if you are about to land in a corn field, it was a good idea to get a bearing on which way to walk out, especially when the corn was 8 to 9 feet tall. It only took one off-landing followed by an impromptu game of "Marco-Polo" to find my way out of the field. I learned the darker the color green of a field, the taller the crop planted there.

Speaking of corn, some of the Kansas Homegrown members found summer jobs working in the corn fields around the Lawrence, KS area. The money we earned de-tasseling plants to create a hybrid seed corn paid for our winter months of skydiving. One year, a couple of us jumped into one of the fields at the end of the season and I jokingly asked the company representative if we could be aerial supervisors. Although he misunderstood my question, the next summer we became area supervisors which increased our pay and from then on, we mostly managed the crews who did the real work.

By the time I got to fifty jumps, I had met many of the local jumpers, been to a few drop zones in Kansas and Texas and gotten to the point where nothing was more important to me than skydiving.

Since I was one of the last students who went through training at Sky High in Desoto, I was getting a lot of air time with Matt. I picked up on his style of flying, which was very relaxed and smooth, much like his demeanor. I learned from others, but Matt's style stuck with me.

As a result, doing relative work became just thinking of where I wanted to go, without having to concentrate on what my arms or legs were doing. Plenty of mistakes were still made, but once we became comfortable flying with a regular group of people, everything started happening very smoothly as if in slow motion; even though we were hurtling towards the planet.

The parachutes we used back then were just a way to get us safely back on the ground so we could get back in the air and do more flying. With today's parachutes, although they have the potential for more precise and softer landings, there is also the possibility of hitting the ground as hard as if you weren't even wearing one.

Picking up on what was going on at the time in southern

California, relative work became my main area of focus. In the early 70's, there was a choice between the classic disciplines of style and accuracy or relative work. Matt instilled relative work in me, whether out of a Cessna, formation Beech, loads on trips to Texas, or even sliding down an icy slope lying on cafeteria trays. Following a unique ice storm in Lawrence, someone discovered a golf course where a few of us (the base) would start sliding down from the top of the hill and the others would start part way down, catching up and docking on the base. We called it ski-diving. Those conditions only happened once and lasted for a day or so. We were always about finding different ways of doing relative work: car to car transfers racing down the interstate and, one time, a boat-to-boat transfer (attempt).

I remember one day sitting in my dorm room at KU. Matt just returned from a trip to Elsinore, California. He gave me a photo of a 26-man star, the new world record large formation. He told me to get rid of my jump boots because they were all wearing tennis shoes. He was very animated which inspired me even more about where relative work was about to take us.

More often than anywhere else, the Kansas Homegrown traveled to different drop zones in Texas. We competed in ten-man speed star events and attempted several 20-man stars out of two Twin Beeches. We got close a couple of times but were never able to complete a 20-man. We earned Texas Skydiver Family status, which we still maintain today.

There were also at least two trips to the largest 10-man speed star event in the world at Zephyrhills, Florida that Matt has written about. On one of those trips the Kansas Homegrown was awarded the coveted God Frog good vibes trophy. On my first trip to Florida and with only 60 jumps, I watched the team from the ground; however, the God Frog trophy resided on the fireplace mantle of our rental home in Lawrence, Kansas for a year.

In the fall of 1973, several of us traveled to Elsinore, CA

and participated in a scrambles event. One night during that event we watched some recent jumps that Ray Cottingham had filmed up in the Pacific Northwest. What we saw was mind blowing! I usually refer to them as the "Seattle guys" although there were jumpers from several states on those jumps, and they performed formations that I don't think any of us had imagined at that time and were a major influence on what we would do in the future.

The Kansas Homegrown established ourselves as a group of jumpers primarily interested in exploring the new direction of sequential formations that relative work was taking. Ron Luginbill from Texas joined us from the start at Casa Grande. He and his wife Barb were the weekly hosts for our dive designing, discussions and eventually the film reviews from the previous week's skydives, usually accompanied with Barb's spaghetti dinner that kept our energy flowing and some of us from starving to death.

As we began making jumps on a regular basis at Casa Grande we would drop our rigs in the packing area, and there was this guy who would land his Red, White and Blue PC (Para-Commander parachute) right in the middle of the grass, usually last, and always made a soft stand-up landing. We thought, this guy looks like he knows what he's doing and maybe he would like to join us. That guy was Randy Deluca. He immediately became a part of our group and eventually one of the cameramen when we started to film the movie *Wings*.

There was a subtle cultural change that took place once our jumps started to be filmed. Some of those early dives would end up with one of us taking out the base, landing on someone's back, and all the other things that usually go wrong when people are learning how to do relative work. That led to finger pointing on the ground, and de-briefs included statements like; "you hit it too hard" or "why did you do that?" and so on. Even before the first films came back, the post-dive conversations started to sound more like; "I think I may have docked too hard" or "no, I think I may have slid under you". The age of taking responsibility had begun.

Since it was on film, we had to wait for a week before we were able to see them, and for the first time everyone could see what was really happening. How spoiled we have become with the advent of air-to-air video and even more so now that so many jumpers are wearing Go-Pro cameras.

The majority of the filming of *Wings* took place from January through May of 1975. Many of those dives were the first time tried or first time filmed. Some took several attempts before we got it right, but when we did there was a huge feeling of accomplishment.

One of the most visual experiences for me was a ten-man wedge at night and what would be the last jump on the film. Matt and I were on the back corners of the wedge and were supposed to light flares on our approaches to the formation. I went well past and below while I tried to light my flare. As I flew back up to my slot, the formation began to glow from the light of our flares, especially Bob Schaffer's blue Jerry Bird rig. I had the impression that both Matt and I came from below on our way up to that wedge.

There was one weekend that we referred to as "the Boenish weekend" when Carl came over and did a lot of ground and air to air filming. One of the original Kansas Homegrown members, Kent Farney, happened to show up on that weekend and was included in several scenes in *Wings*. It could have been just as easily called "the Farney weekend" as he had one of the best cases of perfect timing I ever witnessed.

Kent was a friend of my older brother and when I was about 15 years old, he and my brother would have me sit on their weight bar to add 100 pounds to their lifts. I was surprised the day he showed up at Sky High in Desoto as an experienced skydiver when I had only a few jumps.

One of the most, if not the most, difficult life decisions I had to make was after we returned from Germany in 1975, and the USFET had completed its mission. Things had slowed down at Casa Grande and a few of us started jumping at nearby Coolidge AZ. An eight-man team formed and attended a competition to pick a sponsored team to represent the US at an international trial of the new format of sequential skydiving: a World Cup in South Africa. Our group did not win and we were once again left with a decision of what to do next.

A meeting was proposed by B.J. Worth to discuss the forming of a competitive team that would be run unlike any previous effort: more like a Monday through Friday day job, not just on weekends like we had been doing. Along with me, B.J. invited two of the most innovative thinkers from the USFET: Matt Farmer and Skratch Garrison. Skratch was one of the rule makers for speed stars and had witnessed how competition would assimilate something that was unlimited. The decision was whether to continue pushing the limits of what was possible in freefall as we had been doing for the

Matt Farmer with Jim Captain at The Gulch

past few years or to completely change course and form a competition team that would inherently limit ourselves to a new set of rules. The Kansas Homegrown at times entered different skydiving meets, including the largest ten-man speed star meet ever held and being a competitive person by nature, that was something I had always enjoyed. What took place that evening and into the next morning may be a story for another time…. For their own reasons, neither Matt nor Skratch wanted to go the competition route. For me, this put an end to what could have been endless exploration of things not even imagined yet. As they say, when one door closes, another door opens….

At some point after that meeting of the minds, here is what Skratch wrote about his decision in an excerpt from the Pat and Jan Works book *United We Fall*:

" Nexus – Nexus "

And the time winds wail —
Analyze —
    What teams do to get good —
    With their daily doses of balanced diet —
    Donutize, back-in & hop-over
    The basic ingredients
    And the timing practice for crosses & weaves
And analyze —
    Those special times past
    When the fantasy flowed and the dives were hot —
    The USFET magic was a frame of mind —
    There because we believed in it —
Analyze —
    The quadra-bipole flash —
    And the mood components of organized dives —
Analyze, too —
    The 道 *— the path — the ASC —*
    The jump run feeling of tuning in —
    And that explosive expansion of awareness —
    When you're still going fast —
    And the world slows down —
    To canopy speed —
Analyze —
    Competition —
    The energy trap —
    The price of that edge —
    Is a focus too narrow —
    No fantasy —
    How good a donut—
    Do you really want to make —

Analyze —
  Journeys and goals and equating the two —
  And the multiplex balance —
  Of practice and challenge —
  Focus — variety —
  Choosing and drifting —
  On an edge —
  Not out —
  But in —
Analyze —
  The air flow and yours —
  Swooping and swarming and all that milling —
  Valences — slaloms — infinities — pulsars —
  Lurk loads — maneuver flakes —
  Lounge exits — air flow days
  Demo dives —
  And coordination boogies —-
Analyze —
  Until —
  It's time —
  You'll have to pardon me now —
  But I'm getting off here —
  It was fun writing here —
  Analyzing with you —
  But that's dirt dive offramp —
  And I've a fantasy to do — "

— Skratch Garrison

I moved out of the desert to Pope Valley, California where the 8-man team, Mirror Image, was formed. From 1977 to 1979 the team trained, and with Rande Deluca, we continued to make movies and won two National and two World Championships. After Pope Valley closed in 1980, a new team formed for the 1981 season in Zephyrhills, Florida. Rande Deluca stayed behind and B.J. brought in Jim Baker, another member from the Kansas Homegrown, to fill the camera slot. That was my final season with the team after winning our third National and World titles.

Several years later B.J. invited former USFET members B.T. (Bob Taylor), Gary "Hod" Sanders and me to participate in the opening ceremonies of the 1988 Seoul Olympics. Other opportunities came along as a coach for the Danish 8-way team, AFF & Tandem instructing, load organizing in Bali, Indonesia, Australia and around Europe, work in the television and film Industry and finally as a member of The World Team.

To think that it all started one night in a Safeway grocery store, that led me to Desoto Kansas where I met Matt Farmer that took me on a life journey and a path I could never have imagined.

All in all, I think the Kansas Homegrown did pretty well.

PART 2

FURTHER ESCAPADES

HOW CRAZY IS TOO CRAZY?

Matt Farmer

With the "Edgerton Boys," we had most (8) of a ten-man team so we just pretended we had one and began to make plans to get this "team" to Florida. Initial negotiations with the Edgerton boys revealed that one of their members, Rick Bridges, was a commercial driver, familiar with moving things across the country. They felt the logistics should be left to Rick.

The Edgerton boys were very middle-class compared to the Homegrown and had real jobs and even wives and families. The wives, it almost goes without saying, hated skydivers or, more accurately, hated that their husbands wasted money and risked their lives skydiving. Bridges, fortuitously as it turned out, came up with a cheap small school bus to rent for the trip. Final details were to be ironed-out at a meeting in a popular Kansas City restaurant.

The Edgerton boys, foolishly we believed, invited their wives to the meeting. Bridges started the meeting by laying out his plan for transportation. This was followed by a discussion of details like departure and return dates.

The Homegrown saw the whole thing as another skydiving trip which pretty much meant leave late, dash down, hang for as long as the diving was good and then dash back.

It soon became clear from the discussion that the Edgerton wives had seized on their husbands' trip as a chance for an unexpected fall vacation to sunny Florida. These conflicting visions of the trip's purpose made consensus on details difficult. To move things along, we took to voting on proposals. Unfortunately for the Homegrown, both the Edgerton boys and their wives thought they were eligible to vote, basically doubling their votes.

Finally, after one tense discussion, Bridges' wife leaped to her feet and shouted out, "Well, I vote that we…"

Ernie Bob had had enough. He jumped up and told her point blank and loudly," You don't have a vote!"

This brought immediate indignation and revulsion, not just on the part of the Edgerton wives, but every woman in the restaurant. The meeting was over.

On the appointed departure day, Bridges showed up at the wheel of a small yellow school bus with" Baptist Bible School" in big black letters on both sides. B.A., as he often was, was the first to see opportunity in the situation: "Hey guys, we're going right through the heart of the Old South on a God damn Baptist school bus. You couldn't plan better cover. We can party hearty the whole way!"

Under B.A.'s supervision, the back half of the seats were quickly removed and the beer-stained, roach-burned living room rug from the farm house dragged out and put down in the back of the bus. This was followed by mattresses, blankets, many pillows and even a couple of bean bag chairs. Parachutes followed. Jacque Le'Bong was on the load, as was a stash of blonde Moroccan hash. Several bags of homegrown were loaded along with a small bottle of mescaline tabs. Overflowing beer coolers were wedged between the remaining bus seats and the Homegrown were ready to travel 1970's style. Then it was on to pick up the Edgerton wives.

They made their entrance dressed in their new "middleclass girls on vacation to Florida" outfits and got Rick to move a beer cooler so they could all sit together up front where they became part of the "cover" even though they refused to clasp their hands as if in prayer as instructed by B.A.

On we rolled through Missouri and down into "Deliverance" country. It was late at night when we rolled into Birmingham, Alabama. Everyone, even the Edgerton wives, wanted to pray while in Birmingham (We suspected Bull Connor and his people didn't like hippies any more than they did black people.)

We slipped on into "Easy Rider" country at dawn and just kept going, running now on a vicious Bong mixture of homegrown leaf and slivers of blonde Hash. Bridges, upfront in his teamsters' jacket, drove the whole way, remaining conscious on cigars, whites and truck stop coffee.

No worries. We were in Florida with our ten-man team and ready to boogie. Money was collected for the entry fee and we entered the meet. Evidently all that praying worked because we got a late draw and wouldn't jump until the next day.

A week later, the Edgerton wives found a ride to the Tampa airport and flew home to Kansas City. We never saw them again. It's not clear whether the Edgerton boys did, or not. Rumor had it both ways, not that we cared or could even figure out which rumor to hope was true.

THE DARING DIVER OR
THE VENERATION OF DAVE SNYDER

Kent Farney

It gets cold in Kansas in December. I was a premed student at Kansas State University in Manhattan Kansas facing the entrance exams for medical school. Most of the college kids were leaving to their homes for the holidays. I stayed in Manhattan to focus on the upcoming test, alone in my shared apartment.

Before I could even crack a book, I got a call from Matt Farmer. He and Herb Conley (founding members of the notorious "Kansas Homegrown" skydivers) were going to Herrington, Kansas drop zone for the weekend. They wanted my roommate "Ernie Bob" Johnson (E.B.) and me to meet them for some rare and cold Kansas winter skydives. They didn't have to ask twice; E.B. was as eager to go as I. The plan was that E.B. and I would drive in his car to the remote drop zone 50 miles south of Manhattan. After the skydives, he would continue to his home in Salina another 50 miles to the west.

Herb Conley was a civilian flight instructor working at Forbes Air Force Base and had access to the aircraft in the base flying club. Herb was able to get a little two-place Cessna 150 trainer for Matt and him to fly to the Herrington DZ.

The Herrington Drop Zone was run by Dave Snyder who had a nice five-place Cessna 185 Skywagon. Dave was former military, a KS State graduate, a straight shooter. Honest and by the book, he was a good pilot and ran a straight, by the rules, drop zone. Dave was a devoted member of the United States Parachute Association and was the designated USPA Area Safety Officer.

Our group was considerably less formal. The Homegrown,

being immortal (maybe a little immoral) were inclined to interpret rules as recommendations and were not afraid to push the limits. Synonyms for the group include loose, more looseness, desperados, more is better, derelicts. Herb came up with the name Kansas Homegrown which seemed appropriate and it stuck. There was, of course, tension between our group and Dave (and his crowd), but we all loved skydiving. And the Homegrown were good at it, especially freefall relative work. That mutual passion for skydiving assuaged our wide social differences.

I believe I mentioned it was cold, like in the teens, and here we were at this remote former bomber base in nowhere Kansas trying to skydive. After a blanketing of snow, a cold north wind swept over the plains. It didn't matter to us; we were willing to suffer the pain of the cold for a few good skydives. The only problem was the jump plane wouldn't start. The oil was too thick for the engine to crank fast enough. We tried all day to start the 185. Aircraft problems were not a rare event in Kansas skydiving. Eventually people started getting frustrated and leaving, including E.B.

Now Farmer, Conley and I are the only ones left on the drop zone and I realize I have no ride back to Manhattan. Everyone else is gone and I don't have a car. Farmer and Conley are getting into the petite Cessna 150 to depart for Topeka. I'm stranded in the middle of nowhere; it's getting dark and it's cold. Solution: go with Farmer and Conley in the 150 and parachute into Manhattan.

There is a practice football field right across from my apartment — a perfect place to land. Problem: the C-150 is a small two-place aircraft and there are three of us plus three sets of parachute gear. The airplane was not designed for the weight of three people and gear. Being immortal and fearless we figure we'll give it a try. We have two things in our favor. The cold air is very helpful for lift and we have a long bomber runway. Conley is not sure the airplane will get off the ground but is willing to try given the long runway. Farmer gets into the fetal position in the baggage space on top of the parachute gear. I barely get in with my gear on in the right seat. It's tight, very tight, but we're loaded and ready to go. Dave Snyder is watching this circus from a distance in disbelief.

We start down the runway full power, but still are off to a dangerously slow start. The stressed little C-150 lumbers down the runway slowly picking up speed. On and on until finally Conley nurses the grossly overweight little Cessna off the runway, stall warning blaring off and on.

It's flat in nowhere Kansas and believe me, we need flatness. That poor little Cessna is hard pressed to climb 100 feet per minute, but it does climb just enough for us to head north to Manhattan. By the time we get there, we have the 2000+ feet for the jump and the Cessna is at its limit. It won't climb anymore.

Now it is dark but the city is well-lit due to a recent blanket of snow reflecting the lights of the city. The inside windows of the cabin are iced over from the three of us breathing in a confined space. The cold is freezing the windshield, making it difficult to spot the jump properly. My apartment is on the west side of town with that perfect football field landing zone. When I think we are close to the right spot, Conley throttles back. I unlatch the door and push with all my might against the airflow. When Conley pushes left rudder to slip the plane away from my door, I cartwheel out, my right arm catching the wheel. Over and over I tumble into the cold night air. I pull the rip cord and there it is, my beautiful black and gold PC.

Amazingly enough, I am right over the football field. The wind is blowing from the west, probably 20 knots. My PC has a forward speed of 10 knots. I realize if I turn into the wind over the field, I will be blown backward into the center of Manhattan, power lines, cars, buildings and all. My only choice is to turn and run with the wind to the other side, the east side. Turning downwind I'm making 30 knots across the ground, just enough to make it across the center of town.

I spot a little clearing on top of a small hill with a winding road next to it. I hook my PC just in time for a stand-up landing close to the road. A guy in a pickup truck coming up the road sees me land. He stops; I ask for a ride and throw my gear into the back of his pickup. In minutes I'm back in my apartment safe and warm. Now it turns out that Good Samaritan guy was just visiting and was headed out of town. Tired and hungry, I eat dinner and go to sleep. Up the next morning, it's a new day! Coffee brewing and I stroll out to get the local newspaper. Front page: "UFO spotted over Manhattan!"

Apparently my parachute could be clearly seen crossing the city. It caused an uproar and the authorities thought it must be an emergency bail out. Police, Fire Department, Civil Air Patrol were all looking for downed plane and possible survivors. The news article described me as "The Daring Diver." Oh yeah, I liked the new title (and it stuck with me).

Of course the Federal Aviation Administration (FAA) got wind of it and opened an investigation. They have an old Roman punishment for such blatant violations of aeronautical and civil law: it's called crucifixion. Realizing the newspaper described an unlawful bandit jump, the FAA wanted blood. And guess who they focused on — Dave Snyder, the Area Safety Officer and only Drop Zone operator for a hundred miles. Conley would have lost his pilot's license. I would have been fined and Farmer, well, he would have gotten jail time for allowing this nonsense to happen. And it was all on the venerable Dave Snyder. Turns out we all regretted those nasty things we said about the strait-laced, by the book, Dave Snyder. Even pressured for at least a year by the FAA, he denied any knowledge of the incident.

NIGHT DIVES AT THE GULCH

Matt Farmer

Our first winter at The Gulch, we Homegrowns pretty much stayed with our small group of sequential relative workers unless someone we respected was organizing a large load to break some kind of star or formation record. One memorable star record attempt was to break the record for the largest star at night. Night jumps are difficult and half-ass dangerous undertakings not to be taken lightly.

B.J. Worth was organizing a night star record. He knew that to get the twenty plus relative workers in the air necessary to break the record, he'd need the participation of both the whiskey divers and the Homegrown.

I was skeptical and disinclined to dive out of an airplane at 12,500' in the middle of the night with a bunch of drunks. B.J., true to his reputation as a world class organizer, got the whiskey divers to agree that, for the purpose of record night jumps, they would forego the whiskey and take only methamphetamines, or "whites" as they were called at the time. We agreed that due to the late hours involved, a "whites only" policy for the night jumps was a reasonable compromise. Arrangements were made for the planes and the rest of the load. The jumps were scheduled for the next full moon night.

When the night arrived, whites were passed around like candy. Jacuzzi stuck the desiccated arm up his jumpsuit sleeve and walked around the loading area offering to shake hands with each jumper. The whiskey divers got the whites part of the policy. They did not, however, as it turned out, get the "only" part.

The Wilsey brothers made up the core of the whiskey

divers. There were three brothers, Tommy, Jerry and John, all big burly boys. As such, they were to go out first and form the "base" star for the divers later in the load to aim at. Evidently whiskey made it onto the plane and a drunken party raged at the back of the plane on each of the three or four jumps we made that night.

The jumps themselves were bizarre. The exits were slow. Each jumper wore several fluorescent glow sticks taped to their helmets or under the bungies of their parachute pack.

By the time the last load was rounded up, loaded up, and the plane had climbed to 12,500' it was well after midnight. I was flying late in the load and, therefore, one of the last jumpers to exit. Once the front of the load had jumped, I ran the length of the dark cabin and dove out the open door into the pitch black.

Once out, I could look for the glow sticks of the people who got out in front of me. Once I closed the horizontal distance to these flyers, rather than diving blindly in the dark, I could lay there on my increasingly solid bubble of vertical air and creep up on the goings-on below.

A couple of the best freefall photographers in the country were on the load hoping to get a picture of a record night star. They were equipped with large strobe lights to light the star. When they fired their cameras in the dark, thousands of feet above the ground, rather than a flash, it looked like a bright ball of light appearing from nowhere. In the middle of the ball, was a small star with a number of other jumpers hovering around, or blazing past. After some fraction of a second, the light would vanish only to reappear a second later with the star and surrounding jumpers in slightly different positions. These strobe flashes were the target that night as we all fell toward the dark planet below.

It was a relief at 3000 feet to finally sit up, dump my rag (military 28' parachute) into the night, and feel its steady opening pull. "Survivor" was the feeling, and I was happy to

just drift under my open chute until I got close enough to
the ground to make out something of the desert terrain I was
floating above.

This was the Sonoran Desert with two-story giant saguaro
cacti, so it was necessary to find an opening in the desert flora
in which to land. I was lucky enough to spot one as I drew
closer to the moonlit desert floor. I headed right over to the
opening. As I turned in for a landing, I noticed another jumper
standing in the opening with his chute laid out on the ground.
Once down, I walked over to the jumper and could see it was
Jerry Wilsey, eldest of the Wilsey clan.

Jerry was standing motionless with his feet apart staring
down at the parachute lines in his hands. When I asked what
was wrong, he slurred back that he couldn't find his parachute
in the dark. A classic whiskey diver problem and the end of any
Homegrown\Whiskey-diver skydiving interaction, regardless
of stipulated rules. We did, however, find the Wilseys to be
intelligent, fun-loving guys on the ground.

SMASHING TIN

Matt Farmer

As it turned out, Arizona has just as limited a construction season as the Midwest. It's just that it's the opposite season. As winter faded to spring and spring to the brutal desert summer, construction slowed. Soon there was rumor of layoffs. With nothing going for me but the sure hands, quick mind and calm demeanor, I went looking for a non-construction job that would pay enough to support my skydiving and, if possible, forestall homelessness. It wasn't long before I found a real possibility. I read an ad in the help wanted section of a newspaper advertising the establishment of a new third shift at a local swamp cooler manufacturing plant. The new shift was the graveyard shift from midnight to 8am.

"Swamp-coolers" are a peculiarly Arizona product. If you've been to Arizona, you probably noticed them: big ugly louvered metal boxes mounted on the sunny side of roofs. They are a poor man's air conditioner or, more technically, an evaporative cooler. There is a run on swamp-coolers at the beginning of every desert summer. Hence, the third shift down at the old swamp works.

I headed right down to the swamp works and discovered the hiring criteria were (1) must be ambulatory and (2) must be able to sign your name. I ambled in and signed up for the third shift and was immediately accepted as a "general machine operator" at minimum wage plus piece rate starting the following Monday at midnight. Orientation to be in the same place as application at that hour.

The guy running the orientation seemed excited that almost half the workers who had signed up had shown-up for the shift. It looked to me that half of that half couldn't possibly have met the hiring criteria. Whatever, we all got a tour of the factory and a stern lecture about the dangers of playing "grab ass" around the big metal stamping machines. Having all dutifully foresworn grab ass, we were assigned machines and the graveyard shift began. Soon the early morning quiet was shattered by the sound of big machines smashing sheet metal into big ugly louvered metal boxes.

The way it worked was that one person would feed the metal sheets into the machine, line the sheet up on the register marks and then cycle the monster by pushing two big red buttons. Another person on the other side of the machine would remove the part and then swab the die with a release fluid that looked, smelled and tasted like a mix of hydraulic oil and dish soap. Piece rate pay depended on the number of correctly smashed pieces the two of you could pull from the machine each hour. This manner of pay was (judging from the lunch room chatter) universally hated. Not me. I loved piece work because I could regularly double and often triple wages.

I soon realized it wasn't just a matter of focused hard work (think sweatshop and you've got it); piece rates assume sweatshop conditions. Indeed, their whole purpose is to create such conditions by incentivizing them. To beat the system, you have to come up with little time savers the piece rate boys who set up and manage the rates never thought of. There being nothing I liked better than a little battle of wits or will, it was game on with the piece rate boys as soon as I smashed my first ugly swamp cooler box into existence. The company was going to pay me handsomely to match wits with their never-seen-on-the-factory-floor piece rate slave drivers. I knew I could never win. Every month or so, they'd raise the piece rate, but so what. While we played, I could afford to make all the jumps I wanted and even rent a little bungalow just a couple of blocks from Ron Luginbill's place.

I began the game of wits by breaking the whole process from lining up the raw material to stacking up the finished pieces into smaller and smaller discrete steps. Then it was just a matter of figuring how to save fractions of a second on each little step. Pretty soon those little saved fractions would add up to double the piece rate for that machine; assuming, of course, you could stay focused and aggressive long enough to run the job at a sweating-from-every pore and aching-at-every-joint pace. I could do that, of course; it was my game.

Finding someone else to play at that pace on the other side of the machine was a real problem. Fortunately, like all life's really tough problems, the answer came out of the blue without warning of any kind. All I had to do was have faith enough to hold my peace and say "Yes" when the answer came. Most of the shift was made up of over-muscled, under-educated young bucks. They were of no use to me: they could work hard but not smart; they made mistakes and, worse, tended to fade toward morning.

What I needed was someone who could toe up to that monster metal smasher and, without flinching, match my pace hour after hour through the long desert night. Among the many young bucks working graveyard that early summer, there was one skinny long-boned shaggy old hill-billy who always wore the same pair of filthy farmer john Levi coveralls. He sidled up to me on break one warm night and offered me a drink from his pint of Four Roses. I couldn't be drinking whiskey and running a big metal press at breakneck pace and told him so. His response surprised me. He said he'd hoped I'd say that because he'd been watching me work and knew I was serious about running the machines which is why he wanted to talk to me. He said: "I know I don't look like much but give me a chance to pull for you and we can make some real money together. I need to start making some money to get my old lady off my back. She's bigger than me and mean as a snake. Give me a chance, boy, and I won't let you down."

I'll admit to some doubts but what could I say?

"We'll give 'er a try."

Try we did and within a week, we were smashing metal at a pace never before seen at the swamp works. That old hill-billy could pull metal out of that smasher as fast as I could throw it in and he could do it all night long. I used my money to jump out of airplanes. He used his to appease a brutish wife. We were both happy until swamp cooler demand slacked and the graveyard shift was laid off.

AMAZING GRACE

Matt Farmer, Kent Farney, Bob Johnson

In 1976, we learned that the Valley Mills drop zone had closed and we found a new one in Cleveland, Texas. Cleveland is in eastern Texas, just north of Houston where the climate is semi-tropical. Doc, Ernie Bob, my wife, Mia, and I decided to fly down in Doc's uncle's 182. Flying with the Mad Doctor was always an adventure. This trip proved different only in degree.

Cleveland turned out to be a nice little airport nestled in the farmland on the edge of the Texas Big Thicket. The Texas boys, having tasted sequential relative work while making jumps with the USFET at the U.S. nationals the year before, were now trying to develop a serious 8-way sequential team for the next National Championships.

We had a good time in Cleveland, in no small part because we discovered that each evening after jumping, the Texans would comb the surrounding cow pastures for the psilocybin mushrooms that grew wild on the local cow pies. The Texans had always had great evening drop zone parties, but now, they were literally a "trip."

All was well until Sunday evening when the Texans all went home. Now we were stuck at the Cleveland airport with no wheels, no money and no place to stay. Thunderstorms had rolled in, preventing our planned departure for Kansas City. There followed a hot, humid, mosquito-ridden sleepless night in a small utility shack on the airport.

Morning brought a patch of blue sky. We saw that patch of blue as the means to our salvation. We knew KC was clear and that it was also cleared to the east. To take advantage of the blue, we threw our gear back in the C-182 and taxied out on the runway pointing north. Plan A was to take-off and fly over the storms to KC.

North-bound up through our patch of blue we went, higher and higher until we hit 14,000' where that poor old heavily-loaded Cessna quit climbing. It was time for plan B: fly around the storms by heading east where the cloud tops started coming down. Eventually, we spotted a hole. With those towering thunderheads to the north, that little hole looked good to us and down the hole we went. The hole took us down to 800 feet where we found ourselves skimming along below the clouds in a dark ominous world of rain, wind and lightning.

It grew tense in that little plane. Ernie Bob pulled on his parachute and demanded Doc give him at least 1000 feet so he could get out. Doc knew that a 1000 feet meant flying up into the clouds and that was just not going to happen, so we settled down to look for a road to follow. The idea was to follow a road to find a town so we could land at the town airport. It almost worked.

We found a road and the road did lead to a town, and on the far side of the town, there was even an airport. Doc was turning final for the airport when a nasty wall of black cloud and rain obliterated the runway, forcing us to turn away. That's it — we knew our luck, not to mention our visibility, had run out over what we came to find out later was the small Texas town of Mount Pleasant.

We started looking for a well-placed field or highway on which to land. As if guided by the hand of the savior of all fools, we flew across U.S. Hwy 67, a 4-lane undivided highway with the beautiful wide shoulders TxDOT so favors. It looked, to us, like runway 25R at LAX materializing out of the rain. Doc rolled around to make a pass, looking for any wires or obstructions. There were plenty, but there was a good stretch just upwind of a small cluster of McMansions along the right shoulder of the highway.

Back we went for another look. Doc made a nice long downwind for Hwy 67 while Bob and I took one last look for wires. The selected stretch still looked good, and Doc set up base to a long high final, holding the plane just above tree top level as we turned our attention to traffic. The undivided 4-lane meant we could claim the whole West-bound side and ignore the East-bound lanes.

Doc eased back on the power and we dropped down to claim our place in the West-bound flow of traffic. Once we were in the flow, we could just cruise along with the traffic which was going along at just about our full-flaps landing speed. All went well until some poor jerk in a muscle car looked in his rear-view mirror, saw an airplane flying formation with him, lost it and hit the brakes. Doc saw his break lights flash, chopped power and we landed.

Fortunately for all concerned, the old front-heavy muscle car couldn't hold that rain-soaked wind-whipped highway. We watched him spin once and disappear backward across the beautiful TxDOT shoulder and on into the shallow ditch beyond. Now we were just another vehicle cruising west on Hwy 67 in the rain. We just had to keep it below take-off speed and look casual (the Mad doctor's specialty).

I don't know how long we motored West on Hwy 67 that evening, probably not long. We were uncomfortable doing it. I know I could see Doc had his jaw set hard, a tell every Homegrown knew and hated to see because it meant Doc was tense, something that very rarely happened and you never wanted to be around when it did. The last time I'd seen it, we were in a twin-engine airplane that had crashed and was on fire with us in it.

But we hadn't crashed this time. In fact, our only real problem was how to get off the highway gracefully, avoid apprehension and figure out how to get back in the air with our plane so we could fly home to Kansas. Really, nothing to get tense about.

First things first, so when we got to a likely-looking road-side McMansion, we just pulled the C-182 into in the driveway and went up and knocked on the front door. No one answered. Having nowhere to go, we knocked some more. An eye appeared at the curtain of the bay window. It disappeared. We knocked some more. The door opened a crack. We crowded up on the porch and told the little old lady hiding behind the heavy door our tale of woe and apologized for parking our plane in her driveway.

The door opened to reveal a large, dark well-furnished living room.

"All y'all come in here out of the storm. Who wants some coffee?"

We took over the living room and quietly discussed our plight over coffee. Our biggest issue now was that C-182 sitting out in the driveway on public display. If you were really lucky in those days before cell phones and homeland security, you could sometimes get away with landing a plane on a highway. But getting it back in the air was even more unlikely than pulling off the landing if the FAA got involved. They would demand that the plane be dis-assembled and trucked out. Big expense and time-consuming hassle. An avoid at all cost scenario.

As soon as we had finished our coffee, the nice little old lady who had rescued us announced that she was calling her cousin Keith who was a pilot and would know what to do. We, especially Doc, tried to dissuade her but to no avail. She called Keith and told him the whole story. We figured we'd be seeing an FAA official real soon. Sure enough, a half an hour later there was a quiet knock at the door but instead of the FAA, it was Keith.

He was one of those skinny, lanky old goats who moved like he'd never quit working. He walked right in and looked us over, shook his head and said, "Y'all better get off your asses and help me push that 182 around back before somebody sees it."

That got the whole party out in the driveway without further discussion. Wing spotters were posted. Keith took the tail; Bob, Doc and I pushed. Around the house we went and into the well-sheltered backyard. There Keith produced a temporary tie-down kit from his truck. We tied the C-182 down in the backyard. That done, Keith invited us all out to his ranch to see his Bellanca and wait for the weather to improve.

Off we went to Keith's where he did, in fact, have a Bellanca, a sleek, powerful low-wing monoplane with retractable gear and a top speed of over 200 kts, arguably, the most sophisticated private aircraft of the post-war era. It marked Keith as the "real deal" when it came to pilots.

The other real deal at Keith's was his wife of many years. Although plagued with arthritis so bad her hands looked all but unusable, she cheerfully went about cooking for and entertaining her husband's scruffy-looking new friends. If we'd have let her, which we wouldn't, she'd have done our laundry. But we weren't worried about hunger or dirty clothes, we were worried about getting the C-182 back in the air and us back to Kansas.

Not to worry. Keith was, once again, way ahead of us. The very next day, he broached the subject in such a way that we knew he'd understood the problem as soon as he'd been called and had been working on it ever since. Keith let us know that the local sheriff was not only a member of Keith's church, but a life-long friend with whom Keith had grown-up. Keith said he believed the sheriff would be willing to block off the highway long enough for us to take off, and that under Keith's guidance, the sheriff was unlikely to feel any other authorities need ever be notified. Although we had little faith in law enforcement of any kind, we were forced to admit that it just might work.

The day after the next was to be the day for our escape. Keith took care of all the details and agreed to act as our liaison with local law enforcement at the take-off. The little old lady who had first rescued us invited us to breakfast on escape day. Breakfast was memorable as was meeting the old lady's bible study group. They pressed miniature bibles into our hands and wished us, "God's speed." I joked with them that we were a lot more interested in take-off speed that morning than God's speed, but I don't think they got it.

Keith and the sheriff showed up and told us to load the plane and run it around to the driveway. The sheriff took his car and blocked the highway in front of the house. When his one-armed deputy showed up in his patrol car, the sheriff told him to go up the road about a mile and "block her off." When the deputy left, we fired back up, waved to the assembled bible study group and taxied off after him. When he stopped and got out to flag traffic, we did a 180 and started our take-off run, concentrating, once again, on wires or obstructions.

We all did, that is, except Ernie Bob. Bob, for some reason, was kneeling in the co-pilot's seat up front and fiddling with his belt buckle trying to get it open. I asked him politely what the f*ck he was doing.

"I'm going to moon them!" he said, referring to the bible study group standing at the end of the old lady's driveway. Again, I didn't have a log to hit him over the head with (see Run River Run following this story), so I tried logic.

"True," I told him, "It is risky to take a 182 off from a public highway, but it is down-right dangerous to moon a Texas bible study group while in Texas. Remember, these people are armed, so let's just help Doc get this thing in the air."

It worked. Bob buckled-up and sat down. We took-off and flew north until we thought we were back on the Kansas City sectional. Then, we just flew home. Another adventure survived.

RUN RIVER RUN

Jim Baker

The Black Canyon is the narrowest, deepest canyon in the country — a thousand feet wide and two thousand feet deep. The Gunnison River falls 43 feet a mile through the canyon. By comparison, the Colorado falls less than 8 feet per mile through the Grand Canyon. The Gunnison River has been raging at the bottom of the Black Canyon for more than a billion years.

Back then, the Gunnison carved its way through relatively soft volcanic and sedimentary rock to establish its course off the central Colorado Plateau. Having carved its initial canyon, it was trapped when a huge block of ancient hard rock planetary crust was pushed up by the Gunnison up-lift. The river, the second largest in Colorado, had nowhere to go but down through the quartz- striped granitic block. This resulted in the incredible narrow deep canyon we know today.

As the river cut downward, pieces of the rim broke off and fell into the river below. Some pieces were the size of train cars, others the size of houses. The smaller drainages crossed by the Gunnison couldn't keep up with the cutting force of the Gunnison. They ended high above and provided no good access to the inner gorge of the canyon. What they did provide was hundreds of fast-moving landslides that blocked the canyon, however briefly, with rock and gravel. The result of the narrow granitic gorge, the rock falls, the landslides, the steep river gradient and the Gunnison's size is a canyon that is considered impassible.

Indeed, no known attempt to traverse the Black Canyon was undertaken until the early years of the twentieth century when two local engineers, Abraham Torrence and William Fellows, attempted to transit the canyon looking for a suitable site for

123

a diversion dam and tunnel to tap the river for the benefit of local farmers and ranchers. Torrence and Fellows began their transit well upriver of the present-day Black Canyon National Park, where the canyon is much smaller and wider and the river nowhere near as fast or treacherous as it becomes through the Black Canyon.

Torrence and Fellows believed they could make the journey in heavily laden wooden boats. All went well for Abraham and Will until they reached what today is called The Narrows of The Black Canyon. At that point Torrence's resolve failed him. This is the entry from his journal on that day:

"When about noon, we reached the mighty jaws past which there was to be no escape, a feeling of nervousness and dread came over me for the first time. Right then I made the only discouraging speech that was made during the entire trip, and I said to Torrence, "Will, your last chance to go out is to the right. You can make it there if you wish, but if we cross the river at this point there can be no return; we must go on."

Back Story

In 1973, a group of five Kansas skydivers called the "Kansas Homegrown" began an annual migration to Casa Grande, Arizona to spend the winter jumping at the infamous "Gulch". That first Fall drive to Arizona, I decided to route my trip through Colorado to backpack in the Rockies before heading to the desert. I was a complete rookie as a backpacker and Mother Nature challenged me with a couple storms that I was unprepared and poorly equipped to endure. I survived and valuable lessons were learned.

During that trip, I was on Highway 50 west of Gunnison, Colorado, when I saw a sign directing motorists to the Black Canyon of the Gunnison National Monument. Curious, I turned in and spent the next couple hours driving to each overlook and taking the short hikes to the rim. At one of the pullouts, I read a sign saying: "World Class trophy trout fishing in the river below."

When I arrived in Casa Grande, I mentioned to my buddies, especially avid fly fishermen Bob Johnson and Matt Farmer, my discovery in Colorado. When I told them about the World Class Trout fishing, the hook was set and we knew we would all have to go back and try our luck.

Over the winter, I got a job working at Camp Trails, a camping and backpacking equipment manufacturer. My employee discount enabled me to purchase my first real backpack and other camping supplies. Matt and I started rock climbing using the most basic ropes and gear. We also backpacked extensively in the Superstition Mountains Wilderness. Our first real attempt at wilderness climbing was to climb Weaver's Needle in the Superstition Mountains east of Phoenix. The Needle is a 1,000-foot-tall column of basaltic rock that forms a distinctive peak visible for many miles. Matt, his wife Mia, my girlfriend Sandy and I, using hemp ropes, nylon straps and a few chocks began our summit attempt. With a lot of determination and a whole lot of luck we made the summit and back down safely.

That winter we were totally focused on skydiving, spending every weekend (and all our money) at the drop zone honing our skills in the air. The rest of our free time was spent learning to rock climb. After work, we would meet at Camelback Mountain Park in Phoenix and climb a very tricky and highly exposed bolt trail up "The Praying Monk". The bolt trail is only about 100 feet long but very challenging, as it is almost vertical with small hand and footholds, and starts more than a hundred feet in the air to begin with. We usually summited in time to watch the sunset over Phoenix then rappelled down to finish the day.

Over that winter, Matt and I purchased better ropes and added carabiners, chocks and other proper climbing gear. That winter we became fairly competent climbers.

Early Trips into the Canyon

The following summer, Matt & Mia Farmer, Bob Johnson, and I left Kansas for our first trip into the Black Canyon. When we arrived, we visited the Monument Headquarters at Gunnison Point to gather information on making our trek into the canyon. I remember reading two warning signs: one read, "Dangerous currents, do not ford the river;" the other read, "Watch out for rim rocks." Rim rocks! What the hell did that mean? After hiking down the trail to the small campground below and looking up, we realized that people sometimes chuck rocks from the rim. How the hell you're supposed to dodge an incoming rock thrown from 2000' above is anyone's guess.

Once at river level, we found we only had about 100 yards of riverbank up and down river before the river turned, forcing a stop. The canyon is very narrow and you would run out of riverbank and come to a sheer wall. Realizing that the best fishing had to be beyond the small section we were limited to, Farmer decided to name these barriers, "Geek Stoppers." Not being Geeks ourselves, we promptly forded the river. The section we crossed required that we wade chest deep in cold and fast water. Using wooden poles to steady our way, we got across to a new section of river not being fished by others.

What we didn't know at that time was a dam was being built upriver by the Army Corps of Engineers, and they were managing the flow of the river. We had happened upon the lowest water of the cycle. That first day we made several crossings, making our way downriver and finally finding a sandy section of riverbank perfect for camping.

The fishing was as good as advertised. There really was world-class trophy trout fishing in the river below. We were routinely catching two to five-pound Rainbow and Brown trout. We were in trout fishing heaven and having the time of our lives. At least we were, until later that afternoon when we discovered the water level was rising. It rose slowly at first, but soon enough became a raging torrent, making it completely impossible to escape back across the river.

Worse, the large sandbar we were camped on was getting smaller and smaller, forcing us back to within a few yards of the sheer rock wall behind us. We knew if the river came up a few more feet, we would be washed downstream to certain doom. To measure the approach of that doom, we placed sticks at the water edge to measure its rise. Thankfully, the river soon reached its peak and we were safe.

Safe, but trapped. Being the type who don't file permits with "authorities", no one knew we had gone down, crossed the river and made our way downstream. We felt it was nobody's business but our own as long as we were willing to accept the consequences.

Spending the next couple of days trapped on that sandbar, we made the best of it. The torrent of water forced the fish into back eddies so the fishing was awesome. We caught so many fish we lost count, keeping only enough to eat. Trout became our only source of protein so we were eating trout three meals a day. We mixed trout with oatmeal and fried trout-paddies for breakfast. We baked whole trout stuffed with dressing in foil with lemon, onion, and peppers for dinner and grilled trout filets for lunch. We joked that we were trapped on a sandbar with too much food.

On the second day, Bob was trying to convince us that he could make the crossing by diving in and swimming like hell to the other side. I was convinced it was suicide and was ready to hit him over the head with a log and knock him out if he tried. Fortunately, he backed off. Mia was starting to get a bit stressed about our situation and we thought about starting a big fire to alert the rangers above to our predicament. The men vetoed that idea, as none of us were ready to admit defeat. Better dead than rescued by rangers.

The next morning, day three, the river receded a bit and I thought I could cross by making jumps across a series of large boulders that protruded above the water line. The first jump was from a large boulder over about six feet of water to a smaller rock. I was successful making the first jump but then realized the next jump was impossible. Brilliant. Now I was trapped on a small boulder not able to go on or jump back to the taller rock.

Not wanting to spend the next underdetermined amount of time on that small rock, we devised a plan to get me back. Matt and Bob, lying on their bellies and hanging over the large rock as far as possible told me to jump back, arms outreached and belly flop against the rock. The plan was for them to grab my arms and lift me to safety before I could slide back into the river. If I jumped short or they missed the catch, I was going to get to swim the Falls of Sorrow. That seemed then, as it does now, certain doom. With no other options to consider, I jumped, arms outreached and belly flopped against the side of the larger rock. My brothers did their job well, catching my wrists and gripping down so hard, I knew I had made it even before they yanked me back onto the larger rock, safe and sound.

On the 4th morning, we woke to find the Canyon Gods had smiled down on us during the night. The river had receded enough to make it possible to cross. We waded back and escaped up the Gunnison Point trail.

After that first memorable trip, Matt or Bob would lead at least one fishing trip a year into the canyon. The Homegrown were becoming river rats loose in the Black Canyon where other people seldom, if ever, went. Over the next few years, we had further Black Canyon challenges making other crossings and we slowly but surely explored more and more of the Canyon. Exploration often forced us to traverse along slippery, talus covered rock ledges before finally making our way back to the trailhead leading back up and out of the canyon.

Many more of our friends were invited to join us and as a group, we became familiar with several other watersheds giving us access to other sections of the river. Ultimately, we had entered the canyon from all known points of access to the river. We had also managed, with no small sacrifice of blood and skin, to find our way up and down the river between accesses.

Photographing the Canyon

In 1977, I had begun my career as a commercial photographer and came up with the idea of going back to create a panoramic view of the canyon from the river below. I reached out to Matt Farmer to see if he would join me in the project. Matt had the best skills and knowledge of the canyon and would be essential in making it happen. Matt agreed and we began putting together a plan. I asked the Park Service if, to anyone's knowledge, the entire canyon had ever been photographed at river level. They were certain it had never been done.

Matt was living in Arizona and I in Kansas. Over the summer, we developed a plan of camping on the rim of the canyon the next summer, making nine descents into the canyon and spending three days in the canyon on each trip down. On each descent, we would pack in a full complement of 35mm and medium format cameras, tripods, and other photographic gear. Our goal was to show a continuous view of the canyon at river level from Gunnison Point to Warner Point (about 6 miles according to the Monument rangers.)

Monument rangers had attempted a transit between those points some years before, using wetsuits, climbing gear and a small whitewater raft for supplies. It took them six days to traverse the six miles. Our plan for photographing the canyon at river level was that on day one we would hike down and set up a river camp. The following morning, we would hike up or down river depending on how the light reached that area of the canyon, taking pictures as we went. The next morning, we would go the other direction to photograph that section. Best light in the canyon required that we often spent hours waiting for the moment when the light was right. Once we got our shots up and down river, we would hike out.

We both knew this would be physically challenging so both of us had gotten in very good shape. The first night that we met, we decided to hike out to the edge of Warner Point. Matt took off in a slow jog and we ended up running the entire trail in the dark. We both realized after that run that we were ready. We discovered a small forest fire on the north rim that we reported to the park service the next day.

In preparation for our trip, Matt had studied the history of the Black Canyon and learned about the first exploration by a team lead by two gentlemen, Torrence and Fellows. These men, not knowing what lay ahead, planned their trip in wooden boats, hobnailed boots, hemp ropes, and sharpened rebar spikes to secure their boats and ropes. Their boats were torn apart when they encountered what they named the "Falls of Sorrow." This section of river drops almost a thousand feet in less than a mile. Their boats were torn apart and they were forced to make their way out of the canyon by scrambling up Echo Canyon on foot. They ultimately made it through, describing their journey along the way. They described one section named the "Boulder Pile" that was particularly difficult.

When Matt and I got to the Boulder Pile on our trip, we found an old rebar spike with a metal ring that we believed had to be one of their anchors used to get through. Matt having studied their journey enabled us to experience many of the same challenges as these original "canyon runners."

During this period, construction of the Crystal Dam by the Army Corps of Engineers was proceeding apace. We visited the Corps headquarters in Montrose, Colorado to learn the schedule for the water releases that would dramatically affect the river's level during our stay. While there was a pattern, there was no guarantee or precise schedule to plan around. We had to stay aware and watch the river so as not to get trapped the way we did during our first trip.

On one of our trips, during breakfast I reached into my pack to throw what I thought was trash and inadvertently threw the previous day's film into the fire. By the time I realized what I had done, it was too late and the film was ruined. We had no choice but to spend another day and repeat that trip downriver. Not having food for another day, Matt was not too pleased with me but didn't hesitate to stay another day and make it happen.

We had many other experiences in the canyon. One particularly exciting one was having to rescue two guys who were completely unprepared for river crossings. They had become trapped like we had on our first trip, but, unlike us, couldn't wait it out and tried to recross at high water. Matt hooked up ropes, setting a belay so we could pull them to safety as they floated by, half-drowned. I photographed the whole thing, laughing my ass off as Matt brought them across.

River crossings when you are packing expensive and sensitive camera gear made for creative approaches. Crossing many times at high water, we would take turns free swimming across wide torrents with a rope; then set up a secure belay and pull the other across with all the gear, using our sleeping mats and water-proof camera bags for buoyancy. Keep in mind that the water was only about 50 degrees and spending more than a couple of minutes in the water would leave you hypothermic. Early morning crossings were often done in near dark and very cold conditions. Getting out soaking wet from freezing cold water required that we immediately get moving to get our body heat up and shake off the cold.

One morning, Matt did the initial rope swim and belay set and I followed with the gear. After spending the time in the river getting pulled across, I then discovered I had forgotten my boots. I had no choice but to free swim back, get my boots and then free swim back again. I was cold and shivering so badly, we had to start a fire to warm me. Another lesson learned.

Spending a month in the canyon, Matt and I became extremely good at free swimming the river, even at high water. We found spots that we would just dive in and swim like hell to the other side. We did this so many times we didn't hesitate to cross at areas that no one else would even consider.

Travel along the river is rarely on flat ground. You're mostly traveling over small boulders. Keeping your feet dry so you don't slip was critical. Twisting an ankle or worse was not an option so we developed a plan to keep moving efficiently. Taking turns leading, the front-runner would pick a path allowing the guy behind to just follow in his footsteps. The guy up front had the hard work picking and choosing which boulders to take, allowing the person behind to simply follow along. We would switch about every fifteen minutes. Over time, we got to the point where we could maintain a constant jog. We had gotten in such good shape, we could hike out of the canyon, which normally took two to three hours, in about forty-five minutes.

After each trip down, I would airmail my film back to my Kansas City photo lab and have that film returned in just a few days. Matt and I had become well known by the local Park Rangers. One ranger, Jim Day, took a liking to us and supported what we were doing. Other rangers were not so supportive. They were not happy that we were crossing the river so many times and even doubted our claims of what we were doing. Jim Day invited us to give a slide show of the inner canyon at one of their ranger campfire talks for visitors. We gladly accepted and after drinking many beers, gave a slide show of the river to the large group of Monument visitors attending that night. I even showed a picture of Matt doing a maximum distance piss off the north rim to the delight of all those attending. It really was an impressive stream, and, of course, the scenery was stunning.

Matt on the rim of the Black Canyon of the Gunnison River in Colrado, 1977.
Photo by Jim Baker

During our time at the Black Canyon, we built on our many fishing trips to become real experts on the lower canyon. No one at that time had spent as much time descending every watershed and exploring up and down every section of the river as we had. We even rented an airplane to shoot aerial photos. Being a skydiver, I had no issues strapping myself to the plane then leaning out the open door to get the best straight down view from above. How we convinced the pilot to let me do it was hilarious.

Doing the Impossible

As we were approaching the end of our photography journey, we came up with the crazy idea that we could travel at river level from Gunnison Point to Warner Point in one day. It had never been done before. No one, especially the Park Rangers, thought it possible. Such a traverse would require nine river crossings, several long delicate rock traverses, and six tough miles of canyon bottom. The only people to ever try it, other than Torrence and Fellows in 1901, was a group of wetsuit clad Monument Rangers who took a small rubber raft through the monument at river level. It took them six days but they made it.

Our plan was to hike down Gunnison Point late in the afternoon, spend the night and leave at first light. We developed this mad plan over evening fires camped at the edge of the ever-chattering river. It began innocently enough with a discussion of the only two expeditions to attempt the canyon at river level. The Monument rangers held the record of six days.

We quizzed each other about how long we thought it might take, given our knowledge of the canyon and river. Our latest endeavors schlepping camera gear around in the canyon gave us the answer: it all depended on what you took with you. Take laden wooden boats and you're not going to make it at all. Take a small inflatable raft full of provisions, and it takes six days.

This led us to a serious discussion of what, if any, supplies and equipment were actually needed to transit the canyon. That discussion led us, over the course of a couple of days, to the conclusion that the only gear we actually used to transit any more were our cut-offs and our sneakers. No ropes, food, or any other survival gear were necessary provided you were willing to bet on a run of less than a day. It was a make it or break it deal.

To make matters worse, we checked with the Corps and learned that they would release water from the Crystal River Dam at noon, so the bet was really half a day. If we got trapped by high-water, we would have to tough it out for a night, cold, hungry and uncomfortable. It was completely insane, but we knew we could do it and that we were going to do it. I had even invited my girlfriend and parents to drive to Colorado to witness the attempt from the rim above. I told them what lookouts to go to so they could hopefully see us from the rim.

Matt and I hiked down the Gunnison Point trail with sleeping bags and a few granola bars, dressed in cut-offs and tennis shoes. That night we hardly slept a wink, both anxious and nervous about our journey the next morning. My secret plan was to start a fire so my folks above would know we were about to begin. While I had been nervously laying in my sleeping bag with little or no sleep through the night, Matt rose at day-break and said calmly, "Let's go."

Without hesitation we were up and stashing our bags. As I feverishly was trying to get a fire started (I really wanted a cup of coffee before leaving), Matt said, "F-ck that, let's go."

From the time we crawled out of our bags to the time we were on the run and in the river was less than five minutes. My family never saw a fire so they missed the whole thing. But we were on our way, Matt leading off at a very fast pace. With the high-water goblin already biting at our asses, the "Trans

Canyon Boogie" had begun.

The first stretch was the "Falls of Sorrow." Moving downriver at pace, the "Falls" is just a long series of cold, scary wades into a fast rapid of scattered boulders, with a quick vault over each boulder and into the eddy on its downriver side, and God help you if you miss a vault or, even worse, an eddy. Even God can't help you if the river is too high or you don't know which boulders to choose before you splash out into that cold-cold river.

We both knew how important it was to stay ahead of the oncoming fast water. Neither of us wanted to spend a night without any food or gear. Fortunately, we were in the best shape of our lives, we knew the canyon and all the crossings very well and were completely wired to get this done.

After about forty-five minutes of non-stop fast paced travel, we got to "The Narrows." Here the canyon narrows between two sheer walls to only about ten yards across. The entire river gets choked through this narrow passage. Nobody in their right mind would free swim The Narrows, but we were way-way past right minds and well into do it or die like men trying. As we were swimming through The Narrows, taking great care to stay within a stroke of the eddy-line, we saw our brother, Bob Johnson, camped below.

Bob had pioneered swimming The Narrows years before. He never had any doubts that we would be coming through that narrow gap that morning and was up waiting for us with a fire and hot coffee. We were so amped up we didn't really even stop. He handed Matt a cup of coffee, but Matt, still running, ended up pouring the entire thing down his beard and chest. I stopped for two steps, took one sip and kept on going. The whole meeting lasted less than a minute and we were on our way. Our lack of manners aside, it was an incredible boost to see our brother who never doubted us. We said we were going to run that canyon. Bob took us at our word, even though he, more than anyone, knew how unlikely such an endeavor really was, and he was there at the crux to help us do it.

For the next couple of hours, we kept a constant pace. We never rested, passing through the Boulder Pile and other obstacles at pace. We had only just unraveled a route for safe passage through the Boulder Pile when we photographed that area some days before.

Fellows had this to say about the Boulder Pile:

"For ages masses of black rock had been falling from above, and in this narrow part had got wedged between the walls of the canyon, forming a tunnel through which the river rushed in a winding course at terrific speed. Mass after mass had fallen until above the tunnel rose a great volume of rock. The most likely thing was that [we] would be sucked down into the maelstrom, or dashed to pieces against the rocky walls."

Fellows described his personal encounter with the Boulder Pile this way:

"Here there were deep pools... where we were obliged to swim, into which the water boiled from the caves above and sucked out again through the crevices between the boulders below. In one of these pools, I was drawn completely under water in an eddy. I fully expected to be drawn down into the crevices of the rocks below, but by dint of the hardest kind of swimming, succeeded in getting into still water. At this time Torrence felt that he would never see me again."

Because we expected high water at noon. our goal for our run was to reach Warner Point by midafternoon, take a rest then hike out before dark. As it turned out, we arrived at Warner Point mid-morning. Rather than resting, we decided to just go for it and hike out then and there. We were on the rim in less than an hour--a hike that normally takes several hours. Luckily, we ran into Ranger Jim Day at the end of our river run who verified that we had done it in just under 3 hours, a big improvement on 6 days. Matt and I accomplished something that had never, to anyone's knowledge, been done before or likely since.

The take away, I hope, is that when you hear or read of human endeavors that seem beyond human capacity, don't assume super humans, assume uncommon human preparation, knowledge and commitment.

AFTERWORD
by Pam Bird

I first met Matt in 1979, after he had moved on from skydiving and into skiing. By then he had progressed from novice to ski instructor to outdoor mountain manager at the Sunrise Ski Area in the White Mountain Apache Reservation, Arizona. Now and then a skydiver friend from the past would show up at the ski area to say hi to Matt. Usually some hard partying followed.

During our first two years together, he taught me telemark skiing, rock climbing, orienteering (map and compass navigation), sailing, white water canoeing, wilderness camping, windsurfing, and fly fishing. After our marriage in 1981, we moved to Oregon (with our 3-mo old son) to pursue a dream of sailing around the world. Matt found, bought and restored an old wooden sloop we rechristened *Shoshin* (yes, I know it's bad luck to rename a boat but you should have seen what had been done to her.) The dream remained a dream as we were consumed with raising our child and exploring the magnificent country we call home.

While Bob Johnson and Matt had stayed in touch after Matt's departure from skydiving, Bob really reentered our lives in Oregon when he moved his family there. Adventures with Bob continued, most notably, a daylong sail (Matt, Bob and me) to relocate newly restored *Shoshin* from Newport to Coos Bay; as well as a 5-day wild and scenic Illinois River hike/swim with Kent Farney, Jim Baker and Matt, and a 5-day Farmer and Johnson family Illinois River inflatable kayak trip.

Bob is the glue that has kept the Homegrown together in spirit. Bob nurtured friendships with each whenever he could, and when Matt's world collapsed, Bob rounded up the Homegrown for a major intervention.

Matt underwent cardiac bypass surgery in 2011. Surgery was successful but complicated by a massive right stroke. Five days later, a percutaneous feeding tube placed to protect his airway dislodged and the feeding slurry was dumped in his abdomen causing peritonitis, resulting in emergency surgery to clean out the mess. When I called Bob, he spread the news to the Homegrown, and then he and Jim Baker arrived a few weeks later and took charge.

Bob's first words to Matt in the hospital were, "Brother, they gutted you like a chicken!"

Matt smiled weakly for the first time. Bob then followed with, "They would have killed an ordinary man."

Matt grinned and even tried a little chuckle.

Every day for a week, Bob and Jim would visit with Matt in the hospital. In the evenings, they would cook dinner and serve me wine, and somehow I got through the initial devastation. Months later when Matt finally was able to come home, the Homegrowns staged their first get-together since 1978. Bob Johnson, Kent Farney, BA, Jim Baker and Jim Captain attended-no small feat since they all were married, working and (except for Bob) lived out of state.

I was the "fly on the wall" when these men shared their stories and memories. Their bonds of friendship were visible and strong. The tales were amazing, hilarious, and disturbing, yet indicative of boys becoming men in an era gone forever.

Over the next five years, reunions followed in Kansas and in Texas with much retelling of the adventures. Details were added, sometimes corrected, often disputed, but the results became richer and more complete, until Bob introduced the idea of writing them into a book.

The Seasons of a Man's Life, a book by Daniel J. Levinson about his research, identifies 4 major developmental phases every human passes through from birth to old age. An online podcast, *The Art of Manliness*, by Brett and Kate McKay, has a 3-part series introducing the overall book content, followed by the Early Adulthood season, and ending with the Midlife Transition. Their description of the dynamic and complex Early Adulthood Season resonates with the experiences, the questing, the Dreams of these boys becoming men.

The Homegrown Early Adulthood Season was framed within the late 1960s and most of the 1970s: a social upwelling of counterculture, personal freedom to experiment with sex, drugs, danger, life, love, death, and personal responsibility, in a society able to tolerate such behavior at least to a degree.

Every one of these men became decent, kind, thoughtful intelligent individuals. Some have faced hardships every bit as severe or more as Matt's with fortitude and determination. All have succeeded personally and professionally: raising families, pursuing careers and contributing to society. The Homegrown shared the transition from adolescence into Early Adulthood and in the process, forged bonds that lasted a lifetime.

AUOS TIME LINE

1966   Matt 1st jump in Viet Nam

1967-69 Matt moved to KS; jumps at Sky Ranch, Dick Hall

1968   Bob Johnson graduates HS; meets Kent Farney

1969   Matt jumps at J.G. Garrison's Desoto, KS drop zone.
             Kent Farney's 1st jump, J.G. Garrison's Desoto, KS DZ, June
             J.G. gives Matt drop zone for plane rental and farm rental

1970   Bob's 1st jump at Matt's Desoto, KS drop zone, Feb 14
             Desoto drop zone named Sky High Skydivers
             National Collegiates Parachute Championships,
                 Deland, FL
             Jim Baker HS graduation
             "Daring Diver"

1971-72 Jim Captain HS graduation; 1st jump, Sky High, June 12
             Rodeo demos
             Stinson Gull-wing plane at Sky High
             Jim Baker 1st jump , Herrington, KS, Oct 31
             Oswego 5-man meet
             Valley Mills (Waco), TX Twin Beech – Bob and Doc
             Zephyrhills, FL Turkey Meet with Jerry Bird and teammates
             Herb Conley's death, Feb 27, 1972
             "Beech Burn"
             Zephyrhills, FL with the Edgerton guys
                 ("How Crazy Is Too Crazy?")

1973-74   Invitation Only DZ at Lawrence, KS airport
"Big Eat" at Lawrence, KS
Kansas 13-man record star – Oswego, KS
Corn detasselling, KS
Elsinore, CA Rumble Seat Scrambles –
   Ray Cottingham films of Seattle/NW formations
   introduced to Kansas Homegrown
Homegrowns move to The Gulch, Casa Grande, AZ
Chute Out Meet at the Gulch

1975   Jim Heydorn's death, Jan 4
Wings filmed and produced Jan-May
USFET organized by B.J. Worth
"Smashing Tin"
US National Sport Parachuting Championships,
   Tahlequah, OK
World Skydiving Chmapionships, Warendorf, Germany

1976   "Amazing Grace"
Matt quit skydiving and moved to AZ

1974-78   "Run River Run"

ABOUT THE AUTHORS

 **Matt Farmer** retired from a law career in 2010 and lives with his wife and dog in Oregon. He has also authored a children's book this year about hummingbirds, *I Hum Every Day*.

 **Kent Farney** is a retired OB/GYN doctor and now living in the Napa region of California. He is an avid airplane pilot and also a certified gyrocopter instructor.

 **Bob Johnson** and his wife Nancy split their time between Ashland and Brandon, Oregon. He is semi-retired from his Real Estate career and devotes most of his energies to golfing, fishing, travel and grandkids.

Jim Baker and wife Vicki are both happily retired, dividing their time between a cabin in Mound City, KS and home on Marco Island, FL. When not spoiling their kids and grandkids, they stay busy traveling, motorcycling, fishing, and boating.

Jim Captain.
After skydiving nearly 30 years, having made more than 6,000 jumps in a dozen countries on five continents, Jim is now retired and living in Kansas.

ABOVE US ONLY SKY

Made in United States
Troutdale, OR
06/10/2024

20437957R00093